*The Environmental Crisis
and Biblical Restoration*

TO DRESS IT
& TO KEEP IT

LEONARDO BALENA
NEY MARANHÃO

cantaroinstitute.org

To Tend and to Keep. Published by Cántaro Publications, a publishing imprint of the Cántaro Institute, 3248 Twenty-First St.,Jordan Station, ON. L0R 1S0

Book design by Paul Aurich

Library & Archives Canada
ISBN 978-1-998711-09-3

Printed in the United States of America

Praise to the Creator God*

THE HEAVENS DECLARE THE glory of God;
And the firmament sheweth his handywork.

The earth is the LORD's, and the fulness thereof;
The world, and they that dwell therein.

O LORD our Lord, how excellent is thy name
    in all the earth!
Who hast set thy glory above the heavens.
When I consider thy heavens, the work of thy fingers,
The moon and the stars, which thou
    hast ordained;
What is man, that thou art mindful of him?
And the son of man, that thou visitest him?

Bless the LORD, O my soul.
O LORD my God, thou art very great;
Thou art clothed with honor and majesty:

O LORD, how manifold are thy works!
In wisdom hast thou made them all:The earth is
    full of thy riches.

Thou art worthy, O Lord, to receive glory and honor
and power: for thou hast created all things, and for
    thy pleasure they are and were created.

And every creature which is in heaven, and on the earth, and under the earth, and such as are in the sea, and all that are in them, heard I saying,

Blessing, and honor, and glory, and power, be unto him that
    sitteth upon the throne,
and unto the Lamb forever and ever.

---

*   Composed of excerpts from the following passages: Psalms 19:1; Psalms 24:1; Psalms 8:1-4; Psalms 104:1, 24; Revelation 4:11; and Revelation 5:13.

Table of Contents

Why should stewardship of God's creation be a polarizing issue for many Christians today? Well-informed in both God's Word and his world, the authors offer constructive wisdom on this important calling. Living in the Amazon region, their guidance is just as relevant for us all. If you're looking for light instead of heat, I highly recommend this unique contribution.

Michael Horton, J. Gresham Machen Professor of Theology, Westminster Seminary California

As human beings created in God's image, we have been given a solemn responsibility to care for the world in which he has placed us. This means that we are obligated to protect the earth, the water, the air, and every creature with which God has filled them. This is the message of Leonardo Balena Queiroz in his persuasive new book, *To Dress It and To Keep It*, an excellent introduction to environmental stewardship for Christians.

David T. Koyzis, (PhD, University of Notre Dame) is a Member of Global Scholars Canada and the author of Political Visions and Illusions.

This interdisciplinary essay has been woven with profound intellectual rigor and a consistent biblical foundation. The authors demonstrate, in the light of compelling theological and philosophical insights, that, far from being the instigator of discord, Christianity emerges as a legitimate provider of alternatives for the correct understanding and resolution of any environmental crisis. Indeed, the provocative perspective presented, centered on stewardship and responsible care of creation, offers a valuable redemptive path to restore harmony between humanity and nature. I recommend the reading of this thought-provoking and timely work, produced with discerning dedication by Professors Leonardo Balena Queiroz and Ney Maranhão.

André Luiz de Almeida Mendonça, Justice of the Brazilian Supreme Court.

Foreword

IT IS WONDERFUL TO recall that the Creator delights in His creation. The sky, the earth, and the sea are teeming with creatures providentially made by His powerful hand and magnificent creativity. Not without reason, the psalmist exclaims loudly:

> How manifold are your works, O Lord!
> In wisdom have you made them all; the earth is full
> of your creatures (Psalm 104:24).

All of nature exults in vibrant worship of the name of this blessed Lord. Even the farthest reaches of the galactic expanse—places likely never to be known or explored by human eyes—join the grand chorus of what John Piper calls God's Theater of Wonders.

However, considering the breathtaking beauty of creation, what has been the response of mankind—those made in the image and likeness of the Creator? Destruction. Pollution. Depravity. Nature, as the Apostle Paul points out, groans as if in labor pains, awaiting the final restoration promised by the Lord.

The effects of the fall have devastated all creation, leaving far-reaching ecological consequences. In this confusing and complex context—particularly regarding the God-given mandate of wise environmental stewardship—how should Christians respond?

Why do many Christians consider environmental sustainability a secondary concern? Why is the preservation of God's creation so often relegated to an unimportant place in ecclesiastical dialogue? Why must care for fauna and flora be shaped by worldly ideologies rather than biblical truth? After all, if God, in His great sovereignty, created all things in the universe and entrusted mankind with the responsibility to cultivate and guard His creation, should we not take this command seriously today? Will we allow our ecological engagement to be guided by often-biased popular opinion—or by the eternal Word of God?

To answer these questions, the authors—standing on the shoulders of great theologians such as Augustine, C.S. Lewis, Herman Bavinck, Dietrich Bonhoeffer, Abraham Kuyper, Douglas Moo, and Michael Horton, and drawing also from the insights of philosophers like Herman Dooyeweerd, Hans Rookmaaker, Francis Schaeffer, and Albert Wolters—seek to guide readers in reflecting on how Christians ought to live in relation to the environment.

Through a careful examination of the biblical narrative of Creation, Fall, and Redemption, the authors urge readers to reconsider their role as stewards of divine creation. This work demonstrates that caring for nature cannot be divorced from the Christian faith but must flow naturally from it. In this sense, *To Dress It & to Keep It*, though brief, offers a powerful call to reflection and action, challenging believers to be faithful stewards of God's world and to recognize the intrinsic value of creation, rooted in the Creator's own love and concern for His works.

I recommend this book not only to Christians in academic circles but to the entire church, for the content presented here is vital to cultivating a healthy biblical worldview. In fact, I commend this work not only to believers but also to those who do not identify with Christianity or any faith at all. Allow me to explain: in recent decades, countless caricatures have been drawn about the role of the Christian faith in relation to the environment. The text you hold seeks to dismantle these misconceptions from the foundation of Holy Scripture, revealing that biblical truth is not the cause of our present ecological degradation and crisis, as some boldly claim, but rather its remedy.

João Pessoa/Brazil, November 2023.
Sérgio Augusto de Queiroz
Master's in philosophy (UFPB)
Doctorate in Theology (Trinity Evangelical Divinity School. Validated by PUC-RJ)
Postdoctoral in Human Rights (University of Salamanca)
Pastor of the Cidade Viva Baptist Church

Introduction

"And the LORD God took the man and put him into the garden of Eden to dress it and to keep it" (Gen. 2:15)

THE EXISTENCE OF ART requires no justification by social, political, economic, or even evangelistic criteria. Art needs no justification, since it is not a means to something, but an end in itself, having meaning as God's creation. Although it can perform many functions—such as communication, teaching, entertaining, and contemplation—art presupposes none of them, but rather owes its existence and meaning to the fact that it is a work of the Creator, as Rookmaaker states.[1]

Likewise, nature has value in itself and does not need to be justified by its multiple purposes. To say that something has value in itself does not mean that it is absolute or autonomous, since nothing beneath the sun is free from the dependence imposed by reality, in relation to both Creator and

---

1. Rookmaaker, H.R. *O dom criativo*, (Brasília: Monergismo, 2018), p. 99.

other creatures. On the contrary, to argue that nature has intrinsic value amounts to arguing that nature's importance is not imposed on it by its usefulness to humanity but is found in the fact that God made it.

According to Schaeffer, people who believe that the world came into existence by mere chance are unable to attribute concrete intrinsic value to anything, because such individuals lack an ultimate source of meaning.[2] The existentialist philosopher Albert Camus himself testifies to this condition by pointing out that if existence is absurd, how much more so philosophy and the other sciences.[3] However, for the Christian, it should be different. Since he knows the Creator of all things, it is necessary to recognize the relevance of divine creation, including fauna and flora. However, it can be observed that the Church, in the last decades, has not properly considered the issue of environmental preservation and care of nature. There are three possible, but not exclusive, reasons for this: the dichotomy of thought, the polarization of the argument, and the obstinacy of reasoning.

First, based on a mistaken Platonic perspective, many Christians tend to forget the original goodness of creation

2. Schaeffer, Francis, *Poluição e a morte do homem* (São Paulo: Cultura Cristã, 2003). p. 42.

3. Camus, Albert, *Le mythe de Sisyphe*, (Paris: Gallimard, 1945). p. 14.

and equate it with sin. If the kingdom is not of this world (Jn 18:36) and if true religion is to keep oneself uncontaminated from this world (Jas 1:27), it follows that the things of the world, including politics, work, science, and nature itself, are sinful or, at the very least, inferior, and must be set aside in favor of the sacred things, the things of the Spirit, such as the Bible and the Church. Although it adopts a supposedly orthodox terminology, such a dichotomous view, as will be seen later, is harmful, among other reasons, because creation is belittled as having a secondary relevance.

The second reason Christians face difficulty in addressing the issue of environmental sustainability can be found in the phenomenon of thematic polarization, which tends to arise in sharply divided political settings. Such a phenomenon produces lonely islands of opinion that form an unbridgeable chasm of thoughts and beliefs between politically antagonistic groups. Its first commandment states that it is impossible for a certain issue, if first claimed by the alleged opponent, to be defended in a manner shared by those belonging to an opposing group. It seems that for some Christians, words like "ecology," "deforestation," and "conservation" are synonymous with political struggles waged by rival groups.

The immediate consequence resulting from the above thoughts is contempt for nature, and the further consequence is the secularization of the area. How many groups of true Christians are there who are interested in the defense of the environment and do anything to preserve it? The term "ghostly spirituality" refers to the Church that has no interest in the created world, that is, it does not have a body to exist in the midst of the community.[4] What is the gain of performing charity and inviting others to worship if Christians do not recognize God as Lord over life in its entirety, including Lord over creation?

Thirdly, the term "obstinate" is used to describe reasoning that fails to interpret subjects related to the question of divine creation that are not based on the traditional debate about the amount of time God used to create the universe. While important and necessary, it is crucial to broaden our perspective. We need to return to the biblical text and be reminded of our commitment to the Creator and our responsibility toward His land and creatures. We must question what it means, in today's world, to faithfully honor the Creator through how we live and care for the glorious creation that belongs to Him.[5]

4. Rookmaaker, H. R., *A arte não precisa de justificativa* (Viçosa: Ultimato, 2010), p. 24.

5. Moo, Douglas J., Moo, Jonathan A., *Creation Care: A Biblical Theology of the Natural World* (Grand Rapids, MI: Zondervan Academic, 2018). p. 45.

In this way, considering the problematic situation mentioned above, this text aims, by means of an introductory approach, to align with the biblical principles of creation, fall, and redemption, what should be the behavior of human beings when dealing with the preservation of nature—seen as God's creation, stained by sin, and redeemed by Christ.

1

Creation of Nature

"Thou, *even* thou, *art LORD* alone; thou hast made heaven, the heaven of heavens, with all their host, the earth, and all *things* that *are* therein, the seas, and all that *is* therein, and thou preservest them all; and the host of heaven worshippeth thee" (Neh 9.6).

LYNN WHITE JR., A former University of California professor, wrote in his well-known article "The Historical Roots of Our Ecologic Crisis" that our ecology is conditioned by our beliefs.[1] In other words, how a community decides to behave with regard to the preservation of the environment depends on its beliefs about its nature and destiny, that is,

---

1.   Lynn White Jr., "The Historical Roots of Our Ecologic Crisis," *Science* 155, no. 3767 (1967): 1203–1207, 1205

on its religion. Thus, as a misguided conclusion, White emphasizes the need to detach oneself from the arrogance of orthodox Christianity, which is based on the idea of dominion over creation, and consequently, to equalize all living creatures.

Schaeffer, despite disagreeing with White's conclusion, agrees with his premise.[2] In other words, he agrees that our actions are conditioned by our religious convictions because, according to him, "people do what they believe." Regarding Christians specifically, they believe in the creation account contained in the first chapter of the book of Genesis, which, in the opening verse, states that "In the beginning God created the heavens and the earth" (Gen. 1:1). Therefore, it is not surprising that, contrary to what Lynn White Jr. claimed, there is a strong contribution from the Judeo-Christian tradition, especially the Protestant tradition, in the initial affirmation of the environmental movement.[3] This is because ideas truly do not arise solely from

---

2. Schaeffer, Francis, *Poluição e a morte do homem*, p. 14.

3. For example, considering the significant Protestant Christian influence on the origins of American environmentalism: Stoll, Mark R., *Inherit the Holy Mountain: Religion and the Rise of American Environmentalism* (New York, NY: Oxford University Press, 2015).

intellect but, to a large extent, "reflect our entire personality, our hopes and fears, our anxieties and sorrows."[4]

Furthermore, not without reason, the very emergence of modern science could not find its origin in any other context than within the realm of Christian thought. In the context of the Christian creed, figures such as Galileo, Copernicus, Kepler, and Francis Bacon—all of them, as was also the case with Newton, Faraday, and Maxwell—held the conviction that the universe is the result of divine creation. Moreover, they believed that, given the intelligible nature of God, understanding the truth about the cosmos would be attainable through the exercise of human reason.[5] And, as we will see later in more detail, the Christian understanding that nature is a creature, not a creator, remains valid as an indispensable premise for any philosophical or even scientific inquiry.[6]

---

4. Schaeffer, Francis, *O Deus que se revela* (São Paulo: Cultura Cristã, 2017), p. 106.

5. Schaeffer, Francis. *O Deus que se revela* (São Paulo: Cultura Cristã, 2017), p. 106.

6. For a stimulating and in-depth analysis of the intellectual influence of Christianity on the emergence of modern science: Pearcey, Nancy, Thaxton, Charles, *A alma da ciência: fé cristã e filosofia natural* (São Paulo: Cultura Cristã, 2005).

The Concept of Creation

The Christian worldview begins with a deliberate act of a personal Being who has existed for eternity, carrying out an intelligent plan.[7] It is relevant to remember that the word "creation" throughout the Scriptures assumes a double meaning.[8] It can refer to God's creative activity, which is represented through creative acts—for example, "Let there be light" (Gen. 1:3), "Let there be a firmament" (Gen. 1:6), "Let there be lights" (Gen. 1:14), etc. In the beginning, God, through His sovereignty and power, orders the existence of both visible and invisible things (Col. 1:16), with the universe being formed by His word, that is, through His creative acts (Heb. 11:3). The psalmist proclaims, "For he spoke, and it came to be; he commanded, and it stood firm" (Ps. 33:9). Therefore, the term "creation" primarily indicates this initial act of God's making.

However, the term also implies that God not only creates but also sustains the created order. In Hebrews 1:3, it is written, "He…sustaining all things by his powerful word… seated at the right hand of the Majesty…." In Greek mythology, after being condemned by Zeus, Atlas, the Titan, was tasked with holding the world on his shoulders forever.

---

7. Pearcey, Nancy, Thaxton, Charles, *A alma da ciência: fé cristã e filosofia natural*, p. 80.

8. Wolters, *A criação restaurada*, p. 24.

We know that this mythology, despite being merely an ancient tale, reflects the biblical idea derived from the second meaning of the term creation—God sustains all things.

Similarly, the Belgic Confession (1561), in Article 13 on the doctrine of God's providence, testifies in this manner, "We believe that this good God, after He created all things, did not abandon them to chance or fortune but leads and governs them according to His holy will, in such a way that nothing happens in this world without His orderly arrangement." To underestimate the second concept of creation is to traffic in some form of deism, imagining that God created the universe but then left it. In fact, the same Creator God is the God who maintains existence; creation, from this perspective, being the correlation between sovereign activity and created order (Wolters, 2019, p. 24).

The Purpose of Creation

Having considered the concept, what is the purpose of creation? The author of Hebrews points out, "In bringing many sons and daughters to glory, it was fitting that God, *for whom and through whom everything exists*, *should* make the pioneer of their salvation perfect through what he suffered" (Heb. 2:10, *emphasis added*). For his part, Paul affirms, "Yet for us there is but one God, the Father, from whom all things come, and *through whom we live*" (1 Cor. 8:6, *empha-*

sis added). Finally, to the Romans, Paul continues by saying, "For from him and through him and to him are all things. To him be the glory forever. Amen!" (Rom. 11:36).

The preceding texts unequivocally mention that God created not only people but the entire world for Himself. However, this does not express any perspective of need or loneliness. In other words, God did not create out of necessity but as a self-sufficient benefactor, as John Piper mentions.[9] In his speech at the Areopagus to the Gentiles, the Apostle Paul emphasizes this view by saying, "The God who made the world and everything in it is the Lord of heaven and earth.... He is not served by human hands, as if He needed anything. Rather, He Himself gives everyone life and breath and everything else" (Acts 17:24-25).

So, what does it mean to say that God created all things for Himself? The fact that all things were created and exist for God means that creation exists and was planned with the purpose of manifesting His glory. The natural world reveals this glory everywhere.[10] Indeed, creation is "the arena of God's glory."[11]

---

9. Piper, John, *Providência* (São José dos Campos: Fiel, 2022), p. 70.

10. Piper, p. 71.

11. Williams, J. Rodman, *Teologia sistemática: uma perspectiva pentecostal* (São Paulo: Editora Vida, 2011), p. 99.

The Scriptures teach that "the heavens declare the glory of God, and the sky above proclaims His handiwork. Day to day pours out speech, and night to night reveals knowledge. There is no speech, nor are there words, whose voice is not heard. Their voice goes out through all the earth, and their words to the end of the world" (Ps. 19:1-4). As a result, creatures, when observing nature, should recognize its beauty and respond with praise and exultation solely to the Creator, who causes "the rivers to clap their hands; together they sing for joy" (Ps. 98:8-9) in His presence.

Profound Meanings of Creation

According to Cornelius Plantinga Jr., the existence of a Creator of all things, a statement inherent to the Christian theistic worldview, points to the evidence of "profound meanings" inherent in creation. Some of these meanings, summarized below, are crucial for an appropriate Christian approach to environmental issues.[12]

First and most importantly, there is the profound sense of distinction: the natural inference that there is an immense qualitative difference between the Creator and the creature, with one not being confused with the other ontologically. Just as a painting is not the painter, creation is not God.

---

12. Plantinga Jr., Cornelius, *O crente no mundo de Deu* (São Paulo: Cultura Cristã, 2007), p. 48-55.

There is an infinite God and a finite world, and it is crucial not to confuse them.[13] This dismisses any pantheistic directive of deifying nature.

As a corollary, this leads to the profound sense of reality, which consists of the fact that if God created the heavens and the earth, it follows that there is a "way things are." Therefore, there is an objective reality, independent of what anyone may think about it. Furthermore, there is regularity within creation and its phenomena, constituting "a stable platform for life and learning."[14] Thus, creation asserts itself as a reality with its own structure that should be respected by human beings.

From the redeemed Christian doctrine of creation, one can also extract the profound sense of goodness, consistent with the idea that if God is the Creator, His creation must reflect a part of His character. Thus, everything made by God retains at least some of His goodness and promise (Gen. 1:31), acquiring intrinsic redemptive potential.[15] Therefore, there is nothing in the world that is inherently evil, so that the chaos perceived in any element of creation, from nature to human beings themselves, is susceptible to

---

13. Plantinga Jr., *O crente no mundo de Deu,* p. 49.

14. Plantinga Jr., *O crente no mundo de Deu,* p. 53-55.

15. Plantinga Jr., *O crente no mundo de Deu,* p. 48.

complete dissipation through the effective power of transformation and redemption found in the sacrificial redemption of Christ.

Finally, it is worth mentioning, given the limitations of this study, the profound sense of purpose: created things are unique and often mysterious. Nevertheless, because they are the product of divine wisdom, they are not only intelligible but also filled with purposes.[16] Therefore, human beings can study and contemplate nature, pursuing its wonders and mysteries with a curious and even investigative gaze, but without deifying it.

General Revelation

Given that the natural world was formed to glorify the Creator, nature itself manifests to mankind the goodness, wisdom, and power of God. In other words, God reveals Himself through His creation. This is called general revelation. It is general because it comes to all people in a generic sense.[17] In light of Scripture, such revelation continues, at least, in two forms: conscience and nature.

It occurs in human conscience, as God instills in people an intuition about ethical standards of conduct (Rom. 2:14-

16. JR. Plantinga Jr., *O crente no mundo de Deu*, p. 48.

17. Grudem, Wayne, *Teologia sistemática* (São Paulo: Vida Nova, 1999), p. 83.

15). It happens also in nature, as God reveals Himself through His works. To the Gentiles, Paul states, "[God] did not leave Himself without witness, for He did good by giving you rains from heaven and fruitful seasons, satisfying your hearts with food and gladness" (Acts 14:17).

According to biblical teaching, however, general revelation is insufficient for the salvation of humanity. It is only through specific revelation, that is, the Word of God, that one can come to know about sin, grace, and divine salvation. On this subject, Wolters states that Scripture is like a verbal commentary on a sign language perceived in creation.[18] It is evident that both revelations complement each other harmoniously, so that if there were no general revelation, specific revelation would not make sense to humanity. However, considering that the former exists, it is necessary for the latter to be present for salvific knowledge.

Infinitude and Personality

In contemplating the Creator's infinite and personal character, Schaeffer now questions how creation was accomplished. From the perspective of infinity, there is a colossal abyss. Only God is the infinite Creator, while other things are finite and dependent creatures.[19] Dooyeweerd expresses such

---

18. Wolters, Albert M., *A criação restaurada*, p. 47.

19. Schaeffer, Francis, *Poluição e a morte do homem*, p. 36.

a reality philosophically by mentioning that "Meaning is the being of everything created and the nature of our individuality." For the author, the term "meaning," unlike the usual usage, represents the contingency of the cosmos in relation to the Creator.[20]

Therefore, the human being, the animal, and the plant, in the light of biblical teaching, are all equally separated from God from the creaturely category. If everything that exists was *creatio ex nihilo*, that is, created out of nothing, all things, including man, are equal in origin. Man shares the sixth day with the rest of the creatures; he is made of dust like them, feeds like them, and reproduces by a similar blessing.[21] Schaeffer comments that in the view of creation and God's infinity, people do indeed become one with nature, not from a holistic perspective based on mysticism and pantheism, but from the reality that God made a great unity called Creation.[22]

However, from the perspective of personhood, the human community is distinct from the fauna and flora, in

---

20. Herman Dooyeweerd, *A New Critique of Theoretical Thought: The Necessary Presuppositions of Philosophy*, vol. 1 (Philadelphia: Presbyterian and Reformed Publishing Co., 1969), 4.

21. Derek Kidner, *Gênesis: Introdução e Comentário* (São Paulo: Vida Nova, 1979), 47.

22. Schaeffer, Francis, *Poluição e a morte do homem*, p. 39.

that, despite their inherent finitude, people were created in the image of God Himself. According to the biblical account, "Then God said, 'Let us make mankind in our image, in our likeness, so that they may rule over the fish in the sea and the birds in the sky, over the livestock and all the wild animals, and over all the creatures that move along the ground.' So God created mankind in His own image, in the image of God He created them; male and female He created them" (Gen. 1:26-27).

At this point, Scripture expresses the essential difference between the rest of creation and humanity. Any attempt to blur this creational dividing line is not biblical. It is evident that non-human creation does not resemble the Creator nor possess His image; instead, it has the exact form that God ordains. However, the fate of humans is different, as they were created in the image and likeness of God.

There is a clear distinction between the use of "let us make" and "let the earth bring forth" (Gen. 1:24-26). This expresses separation and union at the same time. In relation to the rest of creation, there is separation in the line: "Let us make man in our image, after our likeness" (Gen. 1:26); but in relation to a single creative work, there is unity in the idea: "God saw everything He had made, and behold, it was very good" (Gen. 1:31).

This understanding of how God carried out creation finds biblical correlation in the statement: "Then the Lord God formed a man from the dust of the ground and breathed into his nostrils the breath of life, and the man became a living being" (Gen. 2:7). The text recounts that, on one hand, humanity derives from a piece of earth. Bonhoeffer (1959, p. 36), in illustrative terms, argues that, because the earth is its mother, humanity comes from its womb, indicating an essential connection between man and the earth itself.[23] At the same time, however, God animates man with spirit, giving him the breath of life in a unique way compared to the rest of creation, as a result of a remarkable "direct, personal, and special encounter" between the divine breath and the dust structure that God Himself shaped.[24]

Image and Dominion

The understanding of the divine image in humanity gives rise to the idea of dominion over creation, so that the first command given by God to human beings is to fill up and dominate what has been made.[25] In Genesis 1:28, it is writ-

---

23. Dietrich Bonhoeffer, *Creation and Fall: A Theological Interpretation of Genesis 1–3* (London: SCM, 1959), p. 36.

24. Barth, Karl, *Church Dogmatics*, vol. 3 (Edinburgh: T&T Clark, 1969), 1.237

25. Derek Kidner, *Gênesis: Introdução e Comentário*, p. 49.

ten that God says, "Be fruitful and multiply, fill the earth and subdue it; have dominion over the fish of the sea, over the birds of the air, and over every living thing that moves on the earth."

What does such a command represent? According to Horton, subduing and ruling creation does not mean autonomous exploitation or violent domination; rather, it is a directive to cultivate and guard the sanctuary in its holiness, drive the serpent out of the garden, and extend God's kingdom.[26]

The first verse of Psalm 24 sings, "The earth is the Lord's and everything in it." This poetic expression indicates two truths: a) the creaturehood of human beings alongside creation, and b) their commission to exercise stewardship in God's world, not as destructive consumers, but as servants. One realizes that it was not the biblical doctrine of creation that caused the oppression of nature, but the sin that came from the Fall.[27]

For his part, Bonhoeffer reminds us that such a commissioned authority of dominion is directly related to our connection with the creatures that are governed. In this

---

26. Horton, Michael, *Doutrinas da Fé Cristã: Uma Teologia Sistemática para os Peregrinos no Caminho* (São Paulo: Cultura Cristã, 2016), 422.

27. Horton, Michael, *Doutrinas da Fé Cristã*, p. 422.

sense, the soil and the animals over which the human being exercises his lordship are the world in which he lives, without which there is no existence.[28] There is, therefore, a mutual dependence between human beings and the world, as "the world depends on us to fill and subdue it, but we depend on the world for our own existence."[29]

The order found in Genesis 1:28 is known as the cultural mandate. This means that, just as Adam and Eve represented the beginning of life in society, the task of tending to the garden represents the beginning of humanity's cultural life. This mandate remains a valid divine imperative for people to continue the work of exploring and realizing the multiple possibilities of development inherent in creation. It should be pointed out, as emphasized by Heber Campos Jr., that this cultural mandate signals that Christians cannot confine their faith to the realm of religion alone; instead, they should strive to fulfill God's purposes in all spheres of life, whether public or private.[30]

---

28. Bonhoeffer, *Dietrich, Creation and Fall*, p. 37.

29. John Frame, *A Doutrina da Vida Cristã* (São Paulo: Cultura Cristã, 2013), p. 814.

30. Campos, *Heber Jr., Amando a Deus no Mundo: Por uma Cosmovisão Reformada* (São José dos Campos, SP: Fiel, 2019), 215.

However, it must be ensured that the cultural mandate does not contradict the need for preservation and care for the natural world, as both directives were given to humanity by God Himself before the Fall. Certainly, dominion has nothing to do with exploitation. While it grants us permission to use the resources of the world, God does not authorize us to abuse them.[31]

Creation and Rest

Walton, in a curious manner, points out that the apogee of the creational work can be found on day seven.[32] It is known that the divine rest on the seventh day does not mean that God was fatigued from His creative deeds accomplished on the preceding six days, and thus needed a day off. Rather, the idea of rest throughout Scripture points to the notion of enjoying security and stability in an ordered system.

For example, by saying, "Come to me, all you who are weary and burdened, and I will give you rest" (Matt. 11:28), Jesus does not offer a simple leisure time or nap but invites people to enter God's ordered kingdom. Similarly, the rest

---

31. Carson, D.A. et al., *Comentário Bíblico Vida Nova* (São Paulo: Vida Nova, 2009), p. 102.

32. Walton, John H., *O Mundo Perdido de Adão e Eva: O Debate sobre a Origem da Humanidade e a Leitura de Gênesis* (Viçosa: Ultimato, 2016), p. 44.

promised by God to the Israelites does not represent relaxation, but rather symbolizes a state of order in society, where the people could live free from invasion and conflict.

When the Genesis account describes that God rested, it represents that the Creator takes up His abode in this ordered system that He had previously developed. In other words, God orders the cosmos for the purpose of establishing His residence and ruling over it, living with His people. The consequence of this understanding is that creation does not belong to human beings for them to do as they please with it but is God's place through which people serve Him as co-regents.[33]

In light of the above, it is possible with the creation account to perceive the astonishingly wonderful way in which all things were created. Through His word God sovereignly calls creation into existence, which is in perfect harmony with all its participants according to the divine purpose. However, it is known that history has not proceeded well; sin has entered the world, creating tyranny, destruction, and misrepresentation of created reality. Individuals go into crisis against their Creator, against their fellow human beings, and against nature.

---

33. Walton, John H., *O Mundo Perdido de Adão e Eva*, p. 48.

2

Fall of Nature

"[…] cursed *is* the ground for thy sake; in sorrow shalt thou eat *of* it all the days of thy life" (Gen 3.17).

GENESIS 3 DESCRIBES THE fall of the human race through sin. The integrated coherence of creation with its inhabitants is marred by the disobedience of the first couple. For Augustine, humanity, apart from God, longed for its own exultation in order to find satisfaction and rushed into pride.[1]

Apostasy and Curse

Adam's sin, as the representative of humanity, generates drastic consequences for all his descendants. The result is

---

1. Augustine, Saint, *On Faith, Hope, and Love* (The Enchiridion): The Early Church Father's Christian Teachings on Prayer and Piety ([S.l.]: Adansonia Publishing, 2018), 14.

that all generations are under condemnation, mired in misery, performing wickedness after wickedness (Gen. 6:5). Paul elucidates this point when he says, "As it is written: There is no one righteous, not even one; there is no one who understands, no one who seeks God. All have turned away; they have together become worthless; there is no one who does good, not even one" (Rom. 3:10-12). And further on, he continues, "For all have sinned and fall short of the glory of God" (Rom. 3:23).

But the devastating effects of the Fall were not limited to the human dimension alone. Dooyeweerd reminds us of the terms of divine judgment, "Cursed is the ground because of you" (Gen. 3:17).[2] Henceforth, it would also produce "thorns and thistles" (Gen. 3:18). Thus, the Fall affected not only the complete temporal existence of humanity but also creation as a whole. Its effects are cosmic. Due to its lack of a separate religious root, being rooted in Adam's, the Earth involuntarily joined humanity's apostasy against the Creator. To the Romans, Paul writes about this dreadful reality, stating that the entirety of creation participates in the drama caused by sin, groaning in agony, experiencing birth pains until now, eagerly awaiting

---

2. Dooyeweerd, Herman, *No Crepúsculo do Pensamento Ocidental* (São Paulo: Hagnos, 2010), p. 187.

the liberation from evil and the redemption of all things by its Lord (Rom. 8:19-22).

Depravity and Plundering

An important point to be made is that sin cannot be confused with creation itself, for all things were created "very good" (Gen. 1:31). The doctrine of total depravity—that is, the biblical understanding that there is no single part of mankind exempt from sin—does not see man as sin, but points to the need for the complete redemption of mankind and its technologies. However, it is true that without transformation through Christ, sin is a source from which sin increasingly flows.[3]

This statement is exemplified by the fact that, when it comes to creation, the Fall does not affect humanity and nature alone; it also affects the way humanity relates to nature. Thus, the biblical understanding of dominion is exercised incorrectly, as Schaeffer points out, and is misrepresented. By creation, man was granted dominion, but as a fallen creature, he has exercised this commandment at will, exploiting created things as if they were nothing in themselves, as if he had an autonomous right over them.[4]

---

3. Allison, Gregg R., *Teologia Histórica: Uma Introdução ao Desenvolvimento da Doutrina Cristã* (São Paulo: Vida Nova, 2017), p. 427.

4. Schaeffer, Francis, *Poluição e a morte do homem*, p. 49.

The distorted notion of dominion over nature is shaped from civilization to civilization, from the worldview assumed by society. In this sense, depending on how individuals understand the God/Nature relationship, they will assume their attitudes towards fauna and flora. Following this line of reasoning, elsewhere we have identified that it is possible to initially identify, for didactic purposes only, three different deficient perspectives on this relationship arising from the Fall, which, throughout history, have led the concept of human dominion and its ramifications: a) *God identified with nature*, b) *God above nature*, and c) *God apart from nature.*[5]

a) God Identified with Nature

The first view—God identified with nature—is the perspective advocated by pantheism. In the light of ecological problems, scholars around the world seek to develop a solution to this problem through the idea that everything is God or is part of God.[6] Here the attempt is made to erase the qualitative—infinite—distinction that exists between God and

---

5. Queiroz, Leonardo B., and Ney Maranhão, "Faith and Sustainability: A Christian Contribution to the Issue of Environmental Preservation," *Findings*, no. 5, June 2023 (Dunedin, New Zealand: Thumbwidth Press), p. 18–20.

6. Grudem, Wayne, *Teologia Sistemática*, p. 204.

creatures. Reality is contemplated as an extension of the divine essence from which all things emanate.[7] In this way, pantheists point out that if everything that exists proceeds from the same substance, the result is that it is necessary to work for the preservation of nature.

However, although it is a view that explicitly argues for environmental care and preservation, pantheism fails to provide a moral foundation for it.

The pantheistic worldview, by identifying God with the world, contradicts the canonical Christian doctrine of creation, which acknowledges the existence of a Creator and creation (Gen. 1:1) and recognizes the natural and infinite distinction between the Creator and the creature. In truth, as emphasized by Williams, pantheism ultimately results from a doctrine of providence (immanence) without a doctrine of creation (transcendence).[8] However, as can be clearly seen, by disregarding the fundamental ontological distinction between the Creator and the creature, pantheism finds itself in serious difficulties when pressed to provide a solid moral foundation to justify its choices.

---

7. Horton, Michael, *Doutrinas da Fé Cristã: Uma Teologia Sistemática para os Peregrinos no Caminho*, p. 42.

8. Williams, J. Rodman, *Teologia Sistemática: Uma Perspectiva Pentecostal* , p. 103.

Moreover, Schaeffer adds that the pantheistic notion ultimately provides an answer to unity but attributes no meaning to diversity. Therefore, this perspective acknowledges meaning in unity but fails to see meaning in particulars, such as in human beings and nature.[9] Consequently, not only does the astounding richness, beauty, and complexity of creation lack a compelling explanation, but the unique responsibility of human beings in their perception and interaction with this environment ultimately also lacks any convincing explanation.

Schaeffer, furthermore, sensibly observes that the Christian understanding of nature does not produce, as does pantheistic thought, an intangible, sacred, or static interaction between humans and the created reality.[10] Indeed, Scripture does not command an inactive relationship (marked by passivity) or a mystical relationship (characterized by attributing human feelings or reactions to fauna and flora). Two situations must be distinguished: firstly, if there is a need, one should proceed as God commanded Peter, "Rise, kill and eat" (Acts 10:13). However, any action stemming from the destructive impulse of human greed must be vehemently opposed and regarded as sin before the Creator of all things.

9. Schaeffer, *Francis, Poluição e a morte do homem*, p. 52.

10. Schaeffer, *Francis, Poluição e a morte do homem*, p. 52

In other words, when the belief in a transcendent, immanent, immutable, and holy God is lost, it becomes impossible to argue about concrete moral reality, that is, about an objective assertion of what is right or wrong. Therefore, any defense of nature based on pantheistic arguments lacks adequate moral validity.

b) God Above Nature

Secondly, there is the conception of God above nature, represented by Platonism and its various ramifications. In the Platonic understanding, matter, pre-existent and eternal, is molded by the Demiurge, just as a craftsman realizes his work. However, there is a distinction between the "upper world," where immutable forms are found, and the "lower world," which consists of appearances and shadows. The upper floor is the world of ideas, a metaphysical notion; the lower floor is the material world, an imperfect reproduction of the eternal world of forms. The practical consequence of this philosophy is the appreciation of immaterial things and contempt for physical things.

The Platonic point of view has influenced many movements, theories, and religions over the centuries. The category he formulated encompassed the dichotomous views of reality, which were opposed by the genuine Christian Church. Gnosticism, for example, believed that—because matter is evil and spirit is good—there is a series of emanations flowing from the supreme deity; those who were closest to such deity would be of a more spiritualized nature.[11]

Later, the tradition of Catholicism came to make a distinction in the world between nature, that which is material and visible, and grace, that which belongs to the heavenly realm. Dooyeweerd criticizes this view by stating that Catholic doctrine failed to realize that the ancient Greek way of thinking was completely immersed in a non-Christian understanding of reality, with a kind of Greek accommodation to Scripture occurring in an attempt at synthesis.[12] In today's world, even within certain segments of the evangelical community, there are still those who, consciously or unconsciously, continue the Greek perspective of dividing reality into "sacred" and "profane," giving primacy to the "spiritual realm."

The understanding of God above nature also accommodates theistic deism, which is the mistaken belief that although there is a personal God who created all things, this being no longer interacts with His creation, presenting Himself as distant and uninterested. It should be noted

---

11. Allison, Gregg R., *Teologia Histórica: Uma Introdução ao Desenvolvimento da Doutrina Cristã*, p. 304.

12. Dooyeweerd, Herman, *Raízes da Cultura Ocidental* (São Paulo: Cultura Cristã, 2015), p. 102.

that deism, on the other hand, results from a doctrine of creation (transcendence) without a doctrine of providence (immanence).[13]

The problem with interpreting God above nature is the attempt to break the integrity of creation by assigning it a secondary character, by relegating it to a lower sphere. Although true believers seek to be faithful through a life guided by this conception, the result is completely different.

The truth is that Christian theism does not accommodate this dualism. From creation, God has a direct and personal relationship with His created beings. At one point, He even engaged with the earth and lovingly formed the human being from the physical-material element, shaping them with His own hands and breathing the breath of life into their nostrils (Gen. 2:7; Job 33:4). The astounding affirmation that everything He had made was "very good" (Gen. 1:31) supports the assertion that there is a special dignity in created things, including those of material nature (such as the earth and the human body), with nothing intrinsically evil in them.

Likewise, as Naugle asserts, the incarnation/resurrection of Christ itself not only values human nature and physical creation but also carries significant philosophical impli-

___

13. Williams, J. Rodman, *Teologia Sistemática: Uma Perspectiva Pentecostal*, p. 103.

cations by dismantling various deficient dualisms such as material/spiritual, body/soul, faith/reason, values/facts, heaven/earth, and so on.[14] The incarnation/resurrection unequivocally demonstrates that God engages with creation in an interested, direct, and even intimate manner.

In the Christian perspective, therefore, there is no room to consider the material world as inferior, nor to envision any disinterested detachment of the Creator from His creation. After all, the incarnation and resurrection of Christ alone provide sufficient proof that the physical and spiritual realities are not opposed to each other or indifferent towards one another. Thus, caring for creation, including environmental sustainability, should not be dismissed as something superfluous in a dark or self-sustaining world, but rather seen as a biblical mandate to be fulfilled.[15]

c) God Apart from Nature

With regard to the Fall and its influence, the last understanding to be analyzed is that of God apart from nature, which is claimed by humanism. Subtle traces of deism can still be observed here. Over time, nature, as conceived in the previous material worldview, is increasingly observed

---

14. Naugle, David K., *Filosofia: Um Guia para Estudantes* (Brasília: Editora Monergismo, 2018), p. 71–72.

15. Schaeffer, Francis, *Poluição e a morte do homem*, p. 41.

as autonomous and independent from grace. The fruit of this relationship, harvested at the time of the Renaissance, is represented by the fact that nature swallowed grace, giving way to humanistic thinking. Such thinking materializes as the system through which people try to find knowledge, meaning, and value, having as its basis humanity itself and its rationality.[16]

People, in this context, enact their total emancipation from the old religious medievalism towards the supposedly enlightened future of reason and science. Dooyeweerd mentions that, based on a proud consciousness, individuals regard nature as an expansive arena of infinite exploration, which will be thoroughly analyzed by total human mastery of natural phenomena.[17] Modern man sees himself as free to reestablish his control in the world through the scientific method, which is considered the only way to conquer nature. Therefore, the humanist, wedded to the scientific ideal of cause and effect, is unable to transcend his materialistic perception, and as a result despises the idea of the divine.

It is interesting to note that the misunderstanding of this view does not lie in the discovery of science. The orderly analysis of the empirical phenomena of reality is not a sin;

16. Schaeffer, Francis, *O Deus que Intervém* (São Paulo: Cultura Cristã, 2016), p. 23.

17. Dooyeweerd, Herman, *Raízes da Cultura Ocidental*, p. 172.

rather, it is part of human life, to the extent that such ability was given by God Himself. Indeed, this kind of intellectual stimulation was instilled even before the Fall, when man was divinely challenged to, through careful and thoughtful observation, give appropriate names to the animals (Gen. 2:19-20)—thus giving rise, to a large extent, to the first known scientific observation.[18]

However, humanism falters when it comes to exercising this scientific method, driven by the unbridled human desire to interpret creation as a mechanistic system that is closed (in terms of the absence of transcendence) and unlimited (regarding available resources). This is precisely what emerged from the misguided dominion legitimized by the thinking of René Descartes, relegating nature to the cold status of an object in service to human interests.[19] This inordinate desire for control over the natural world opens the door to a mistaken understanding since it does not recognize nature as an end in itself for the glory of the Creator. Rather, nature's existence is objectified in light of humanity's covetous purposes. Consequently, Édis Milaré is right when

---

18. Campos, Heber Carlos de, *O Habitat Humano: O Paraíso Criado* (São Paulo: Hagnos, 2011),p. 89–90.

19. Descartes, René, *Discurso do Método*, 3rd ed. (São Paulo: Abril Cultural, 1983), 63.

he highlights that this immoderate human spirit has led to the lamentable "objectification" of nature and its wonders.[20]

In a certain sense, according to Bonhoeffer, it can be said that the very idea of human dominion over nature after the Fall becomes an illusion because it is humanity that is being dominated.[21] As C. S. Lewis aptly puts it, "every new power won by man is a power over man," so that "man is both the conqueror and the captive, the general who conquers and the slave who follows the triumphal car."[22] It is these unrestrained desires for consumption and destruction that imprison him in a vicious cycle of greedy exploitation. The reason we cannot govern properly lies in the fact that we do not recognize the world as God's creation and do not accept the dominion we have as something given by Him. Instead, we appropriate this dominion for ourselves.

Indeed, there is a severe problem of rebellion in the human heart that stems from sin. The equivalence between the creational concept of human dominion and the fallen vision of unlimited exploitation of the environment begins in hu-

---

20. Milaré, Édis, *Direito do Ambiente*, 9th ed. (São Paulo: Editora Revista dos Tribunais, 2014), p. 107.

21. Dietrich Bonhoeffer, *Creation and Fall: A Theological Interpretation of Genesis 1–3*, p. 78.

22. Lewis, C. S., *A Abolição do Homem* (São Paulo: Martins Fontes, 2005), p. 56.

manism, i.e., the perspective of God apart from nature. Thus, the above views, however well-intentioned, are insufficient because they fail to establish a solid and coherent foundation for the preservation and sustainability of creation. There must be a valid alternative.

3

Redemption of Nature

"[...] because the creature itself also shall be delivered from the bondage of corruption into the glorious liberty of the children of God" (Rom 8:21).

THE CHRISTIAN VIEW REGARDING care for nature can be introduced from what Paul writes to the Romans: "For the creation waits in eager expectation for the children of God to be revealed. For the creation was subjected to frustration, not by its own choice, but by the will of the one who subjected it, in hope that the creation itself will be liberated from its bondage to decay and brought into the freedom and glory of the children of God" (Rom. 8:19-21).

New Heaven and New Earth

The text states that when the resurrection of the dead takes place, man and nature will be redeemed together, that is, the blood of the Lamb will also save nature from the captivity of the Fall into sin, resulting in a new heaven and a new earth. As Bavinck highlights, there is a close spiritual connection between the human race and the earth. Both were created in harmony, both subjected to vanity/corruption through the Fall, and both have been redeemed by Christ. Furthermore, both will be glorified together in the future.[1]

We can perceive that the new heaven and the new earth promised by the Lord will be a continuation following the purification through fire of the creation we know today.[2] The hope for the liberation of creation that Paul expresses in Romans 8 implies that the destiny of the natural world is not destruction but transformation. However, this hope for a transformed world encounters some tension with certain passages in the New Testament that seem to announce that the last days will introduce a completely new world with no connection to the old.[3] The passages most commonly used

1. Bavinck, Herman, *As Maravilhas de Deus* (Rio de Janeiro: Thomas Nelson Brasil, 2021),p. 324.

2. Wolters, Albert M., *A Criação Restaurada: A Base Bíblica para uma Cosmovisão Reformada*, p. 53.

3. Moo, Douglas J., "Nature in the New Creation: New Testament Eschatology and the Environment," *Journal of the Evangelical Theological Society* 49, no. 3 (2006): p. 6.

for this purpose are 2 Peter 3:10 and Revelation 21:1. We shall examine both.

In 2 Peter 3:10, it is written, "But the day of the Lord will come like a thief, and then the heavens will pass away with a roar, and the heavenly bodies will be burned up and dissolved, and the earth and the works that are done on it will be exposed." Unfortunately, based on a mistaken notion, some argue that since the known world will be annihilated by fire at the second coming of Christ, there is no need for care or preservation regarding nature. A similar argument is made with the text in Revelation 21:1, "Then I saw a new heaven and a new earth, for the first heaven and the first earth had passed away, and the sea was no more."

In light of the verses mentioned, how can we resolve the apparent tension between the expectation of transformation of the present world and the expectation of destruction and replacement by a new one? Should we consider this language as direct and literal descriptions of a future physical reality, or could John and Peter be using metaphors to depict an eruption of God's power to transform the world as we know it? A detailed analysis of these passages suggests that what is visualized is not annihilation and new creation but rather a radical transformation.[4] John Calvin himself reject-

---

4. Moo, Douglas J., "Nature in the New Creation: New Testament Eschatology and the Environment," p. 6.

ed annihilationist perspectives in favor of purified renewal, believing that the substance of natural elements would remain the same while being renewed.[5]

The interpretation of both passages, as highlighted by Douglas Moo, is complicated by their apocalyptic style, which is characterized by metaphorical language. Starting with Revelation, we see that the original text may refer to judgment instead of destruction. The term used in 21:1 about "passing away" could indicate that it is the sinful "form" of this world that is about to disappear, rather than the world itself. We also see other clues in this context regarding the idea of renewal. In Revelation 21:5, God proclaims, "Behold, I am making all things new!" and not "Behold, I am making all new things." The language here suggests renewal, not destruction and recreation.[6]

Similarly, the text found in 2 Peter may portray a metaphor related to God's final judgment on humanity. The term used in the original related to the understanding of destruction does not necessarily mean total physical annihilation but rather a radical change in their nature. We should remember that the language of destruction often mentioned in the New Testament regarding the eternal fate of those

---

5. Calvino, João, *Epístolas Gerais* (São José dos Campos: Fiel, 2015), p. 224.

6. Moo, Douglas J., "Nature in the New Creation: New Testament Eschatology and the Environment," p.224.

who have rejected the Lord does not mean that such people will be, so to speak, destroyed or annihilated but that they will suffer the condemnation of divine judgment. [7]Hence the correctness of N. T. Wright's lesson, as follows:

> In various parts of the world, Christians are being drawn to a vision of the future that appeals to the final destruction of the created order and to a purely 'spiritual' destiny, in the sense of being completely non-material. This popular perception has persisted both inside and outside the church and is supposedly the view of Christians regarding 'heaven' and the hope we have in Christ. Contrary to these popular and mistaken views, Christianity declares that the work that God the Creator has done in Jesus Christ, and above all in his resurrection, is the same work he desires to do for the entire world – 'world' in the sense of the whole cosmos, with all its history. (…) The transition from the present world to the new one represents not the destruction of the present universe of space/time, but its radical healing.[8]

---

7. Moo, Douglas J., "Nature in the New Creation: New Testament Eschatology and the Environment," p. 6.

8. Wright, N. T., *Surpreendido pela Esperança (Viçosa: Ultimato*, 2009), 107, 138.

In the same vein, Herman Bavinck teaches that, just as man himself is not annihilated but recreated in Christ (2 Corinthians 5:17), "the world, in its essence, will be preserved, although it undergoes such a great change that it is called new heavens and a new earth."[9] Michael Horton also follows this perspective, stating that the idea of a new heaven and a new earth "is not the abolition of the old creation but describes the new condition of the world that the Father made and remade in His Son and through His Spirit."[10] Similarly, J. Rodman Williams notes that "the meaning of this description is not the annihilation of the heavens and the earth but a dissolution, although not total," to the extent that "a renewal will occur, giving new form to the current world."[11]

However, it is noteworthy that regardless of the interpretation chosen for the texts cited, using them as an excuse for Christian inaction regarding the protection of the natural world does not follow the biblical ethical principles pres-

---

9. Bavink, Herman, *As Maravilhas de Deus* (Rio de Janeiro: Thomas Nelson Brasil, 2021), p. 672.

10. Horton, Michael, *Doutrinas da Fé Cristã: Uma Teologia Sistemática para os Peregrinos no Caminho* (São Paulo: Cultura Cristã, 2016), p. 1.018.

11. Williams, J. Rodman, *Teologia Sistemática: Uma Perspectiva Pentecostal* (São Paulo: Editora Vida, 2011), p. 1.156.

ent in the creational order of "tending to and keeping" God's creation. After all, as emphasized by C. S. Lewis, "the Christians who did the most for the present world were just those who thought most of the next."[12] Indeed, if the idea that everything will be destroyed represents the consequent detachment of the believer from such an object, how could we advocate for the pursuit of the restoration of the lordship of Christ over all areas of human life, as we will see later on?

Comprehensive and Immediate Redemption

However, the biblical idea of redemption, although it has a future-oriented dimension as demonstrated in the preceding passage, produces, in the same way, practical consequences for the here and now. According to the famous quote by Kuyper, there is not a single square inch in all the domains of existence over which Christ cannot claim His absolute lordship.[13]

It is understood, therefore, that the extent of redemption in Christ is as wide as the extent of the effects of the Fall, and there is no area so deformed that it cannot be redeemed by the action of divine providence. Let it be reiterated: according to Scripture, when the Lord Jesus shed

12. Lewis, C. S., *Cristianismo Puro e Simples*, 3rd ed. (São Paulo: Editora WMF Martins Fontes, 2009), p. 178.

13. Bratt, James D., *Sphere Sovereignty* (Grand Rapids, MI: Eerdmans, 1988), p. 488.

His blood on the cross of Calvary, He provided not only salvation for souls but indeed for the reconciliation of "all things, whether on earth or in heaven" (Colossians 1:20). In other words, "God was in Christ reconciling the world to Himself" (2 Corinthians 5:19), placing "all things under His feet" (Ephesians 1:21-22). It is not surprising: if the effects of the Fall were cosmic, the scope of redemption in Christ must also be cosmic.

In fact, as Cornelius Plantinga Jr. emphasizes, the entire world belongs to God, and the whole world has fallen; therefore, the whole world needs to be redeemed, which is why God provides salvation not only for human beings but also for social systems and economic structures, including "the whole natural world, which both sings and groans."[14] We must not forget that transforming people transforms cultures.[15]

In other words, the messianic redemption is not limited to saving individuals but encompasses the entire creation. This means we are called to lovingly and wisely promote the restoration of all areas of life, including our relationship with nature. In truth, redemption authorizes us to reclaim the blessed mission given to the first human beings at the beginning of Creation: to lovingly subdue the Earth and ex-

---

14. Plantinga Jr., *O crente no mundo de Deu*, p. 100.

15. Pearcey, Nancy, Thaxton, *Charles, A alma da ciência: fé cristã e filosofia natural*, p. 351.

tend the Creator's dominion over all life.[16] An important point to be noted, however, concerns the fact that, although we should labor diligently to restore Christ's Lordship over all things, the complete and exhaustive redemption of reality will not be fully realized in the present age but will occur in its fullness only at the second coming of the Messiah.

God as the Lord of Nature

The alternative proposed by Christianity to restore the view of man in relation to the environment does not come from any of the three notions presented above, because all of them are the fruit of a mistaken discernment of God that produces an erroneous understanding of creation. The Christian interpretation of the God/Nature relationship could be none other than the one that defends the view of God as the Lord of nature. This expression moves away from the previous problems mentioned by competing perspectives by revealing the sovereignty of the Creator and the need for stewardship by human beings, recognizing that they are not the masters of nature but rather act as vice-regents of the Creator of the Universe.[17]

---

16. Pearcey, Nancy, Thaxton, *Charles, A alma da ciência: fé cristã e filosofia natural*, p. 333-334.

17. Williams, J. *Rodman, Teologia Sistemática: Uma Perspectiva Pentecostal*, p. 174.

However, the reality is that there is a wealth of accusations by scientists that the Judeo-Christian worldview justifies the unrestrained exploitation of nature, making it largely responsible for the alleged environmental crisis. The inquiry into the causes of the environmental problem led Lynn White Jr., then a professor at the University of California, to argue that the ecological crisis is a "failure of Christianity," as he believed that Christian thought has always taught "that man has dominion over nature and, consequently, man has treated nature in a destructive way."[18]

Arnold Joseph Toynbee, for his part, is said to have stated that "Christianity drained divinity from nature."[19] In the same vein, Édis Milaré claims that "the Judeo-Christian tradition reinforces this position of supposed absolute and unquestionable human supremacy over all other beings."[20] Along the same lines, Peter Singer asserts that "God has given humans dominion over the natural world, and God does not care how we treat it."[21]

18. Lynn White Jr., "The Historical Roots of Our Ecologic Crisis," p. 1.206.

19. Beltrão, Antônio Figueiredo Guerra, *Curso de Direito Ambiental*, 2nd ed. (São Paulo: Método, 2014), p. 11.

20. Milaré, *Édis, Direito do Ambiente*, p. 106.

21. Singer, Peter, *Vida Ética (Rio de Janeiro: Ediouro*, 2002) p. 121.

These assertions arise, in part, because the canonical Christian perspective on the relationship between humans and nature has been widely misunderstood. Basically, two biblical passages from the book of Genesis are pointed out as the "pivots" of the problem. The first is Genesis 1:28, which states, "And God blessed them. And God said to them, 'Be fruitful and multiply and fill the earth and subdue it and have dominion over the fish of the sea and over the birds of the heavens and over every living thing that moves on the earth.'" The second is Genesis 2:15, which reads: "The Lord God took the man and put him in the Garden of Eden to work it and keep it."

It is important to note that the command to subdue, have dominion, cultivate, and keep the "garden" was given in a pre-Fall context, that is, before humanity disobeyed God, which only occurred in Genesis 3. In other words, the command to cultivate and keep the garden demonstrates, in light of biblical revelation, the ongoing need to maintain order and balance in all created things. From the very beginning God was concerned with preserving the ecology of the garden, which was to be cultivated and maintained in a proper and suitable manner, a special task that fell upon humankind (the human race).[22] As already emphasized, this

---

22. Campos, Heber Carlos de, *O Habitat Humano: O Paraíso Criado*, p.87.

special human responsibility stems from the unique dignity that humans possess, having been created in the image of God, which primarily means the benevolent ability to choose to do good.[23]

Regarding this specific and controversial point of the asserted special human dignity, it is worth noting that, although coming from somewhat different foundations, this particular responsibility of humankind towards nature and other beings is also reinforced by authors of the caliber of François Ost, as follows:

> For better or worse, we are now responsible for nature, which we are modifying ever more profoundly. It is impossible to escape this historical situation [...]. On the ethical level, the faculty of universalization makes man the only moral subject in the Universe. Because he can 'act otherwise,' because he is free by nature, man is capable of evil; likewise, he is capable of good and even better. In this dual capacity, the ethical law is justified. If he were not capable of self-determination, a moral law would be useless; his behavior, like the course of the stars, would reveal necessity and not morality. On

---

23. Pearcey, Nancy, Thaxton, *Charles, A alma da ciência: fé cristã e filosofia natural*, p. 185-186.

the other hand, since good and even better are within his reach, the moral law is not only relevant but desirable.[24]

However, considering everything that has been explained, it is important to reaffirm that while it is true that the environment does not protect itself, it is also not merely an instrument for human well-being.[25] Therefore, it is highly relevant to quote the insightful explanation of Sérgio Augusto de Queiroz, as follows:

> The meaning behind this ecological-cultural mandate given to man and woman at the moment of creation is that the only beings endowed with rationality, critical thinking, and the capacity for holistic environmental management would be true representatives of the Creator in the process of sustainable development, where the supply of human needs would be balanced with careful care for the environment. It is also interesting to note that in the same chapter of the book of Genesis, the Cre-

---

24. Ost, François, *A Natureza à Margem da Lei: A Ecologia à Prova do Direito* (Lisboa: Instituto Piaget, 1995), p. 233, 249.

25. Gomes, Carla Amado, *Direito Ambiental: O Ambiente como Objeto e os Objetos do Direito do Ambiente* (Curitiba: Juruá, 2010), p. 20.

ator blessed man and woman and commanded them to subdue the Earth. Here, the practical meaning of subduing is to responsibly manage all the resources present in the environment and develop all its potentialities for the glory of God and for the good of all humanity. Thus, to rule and subdue cannot be irrational attitudes that disregard the very seal of the Creator's image in every human being. Therefore, in the Judeo-Christian perspective, care for the environment has a motivation that transcends a merely anthropocentric view and rests on a principle of reverence, respect, and love for the Creator and all of His creation.[26]

It is clear that biblically, man has dominion but not sovereignty. His dominion is functionalized for purposes that are superior to him. Such dominion does not allow degradation, excessive exploitation, or abuse. In this light, man's dominion is only legitimate when practiced in fidelity to God's dominion. After all, from the Christian perspective and as

---

26. Queiroz, Sérgio Augusto de, "O Direito Ambiental e a Cosmovisão Judaico-Cristã," in *Direito e Cristianismo: Temas Atuais e Polêmicos*, vol. 2, coordinated by Abner de Cássio Ferreira, Antonio Carlos da Rosa Silva Júnior, *Glauco Barreira Magalhães Filho, Ney Maranhão, and Rodolfo Pamplona Filho* (Rio de Janeiro: Editora Betel, 2016), p.157.

taught by Francis Schaeffer, nature does not belong to us but to God, which is why we should exercise our dominion over these things "not as if we were meant to exploit them, but as borrowed or entrusted to us," because "man's dominion is under God's dominion."[27]

Dominion, Love, and Balance

To convey the depth of the redeemed Christian thought—because, as stated above, it is this perspective that has been pointed out as the legitimizing factor behind the blind anthropocentrism that has led us to the current ecological crisis—it is worth mentioning that the great characteristic of divine love is precisely the fact that it is governed more by the desire to give than to receive. Indeed, God needs nothing; He did not create to receive, but to give.[28]

The ultimate expression of this love is portrayed by the sacrificial gift of His own Son to redeem flawed and sinful human beings (John 3:16). And according to the Scriptures, becoming a child of God does not mean gaining a new social status, but being the bearer of glorious spiritual power (John 1:11-12), the exercise of which, to remain faithful to God's purposes, must always be practiced with love and

---

27. Schaeffer, Francis, *Poluição e a morte do homem*, p. 48.

28. Williams, J. *Rodman, Teologia Sistemática: Uma Perspectiva Pentecostal*, p. 99.

self-control. That is why the Apostle Paul affirms that "God gave us a spirit not of fear but of power and love and self-control" (2 Timothy 1:7).

Therefore, for the genuine Christian dominion, and in the precise terms of biblical axiology, any dominion should always be practiced with love and balance. Hence, dominion, love, and balance emerge as inseparable dimensions of their faith practice, demonstrating an anthropocentrism that, it is easy to see, steers clear of any tyranny, arbitrariness, or lack of control. It is a qualified anthropocentrism carrying a high ethical dimension and granting mankind a truly distinct dignity within the created order, without losing sight of the sobriety and love that flow from their Creator. As García Rubio aptly teaches, let us consider:

> Indeed, the world existed before the creation of man. It is true that God entrusts it to the care of humanity to 'cultivate and keep' (Gen 2:15), but above all, the created world is a free gift, not made by man. The world, created by the Spirit and the Word of Yahweh, belongs to Him and not to man. As a consequence, human beings should receive it as a gift, rejecting the temptation to consider themselves owners and seeking to take the place of God. Degrading, destroying animal and plant species, polluting the air... is to con-

sider the world as property, it is a senseless and arrogantly foolish attitude. Even more profoundly: it is an attitude that [...] crystallizes today in modes of production-consumption with enormous social and ecological costs.[29]

In light of these considerations, Maranhão labels this perspective as "solidary anthropocentrism," contrasting it with humanistic worldviews. Thus, in the biblical-Christian perspective, the genuine meaning of "dominion" and "subjection" is far from the oppressive and truculent traits that immediately come to mind due to contemporary culture.[30]

It is worth recalling that love is the bond of perfection (Colossians 3:14). Therefore, from a Christian perspective, love—not fear, pleasure, pride, or security—should be the primary motivating factor in our relationship with the environment and, consequently, in the pursuit of solutions to the environmental issue. This love is primarily directed towards God as the Creator of all things (Matthew 22:37). For instance, Roger Scruton advocates for the shared love for

---

29. Rubio, A. García, "Crise Ambiental e Projeto Bíblico de Humanização Integral," in *Reflexão Cristã sobre o Meio Ambiente*, by A. García Rubio et al. (São Paulo: Edições Loyola, 1992), p. 15.

30. Maranhão, Ney, *Poluição Labor-Ambiental* (Rio de Janeiro: Lumen Juris, 2017), p. 85.

our home (*oikophilia*) as an appropriate motive for addressing the environmental cause.[31] It is an interesting intellectual development of a logic of action rooted in love.

The Intrinsic Value of Nature

However, it is necessary to underline that the consequences of something should not be confused with its foundation, lest over time we forget the true reason that thing is done. The redeemed Christian view of God as the Lord of nature, although it produces beneficial effects, does not argue that care for environmental preservation is primarily justified based on the positive results it brings to humans. On the contrary, the foundation of this perspective for caring for nature and everything in it lies in the simple fact that God created it and cares for His creation, granting humanity the mandate to steward and honor it. In other words, sincere Christian ethics presuppose benevolence towards creation.

Nature should be respected and protected primarily because it possesses intrinsic value, as a vital complex that predates us and to which we are invariably connected, that accompanies us throughout our existential journey and presents itself before us with all its grand beauty and unfath-

---

31. Scruton, Roger, *Filosofia Verde: Como Pensar Seriamente o Planeta* (São Paulo: É Realizações, 2016), p. 28–29.

omable mysteries, demanding from us the utmost respect and solidarity as worthy measures of a truly sensible and balanced humanity, conscious of its turbulent limitations and eternal dependence.

It should be noted that the presence of the Spirit at both ends of the biblical narrative of creation (Genesis 1:2 and 2:7; Job 33:4), still active today to sustain it (Psalm 104:30; Job 34:14-15), demonstrates a prodigious and fascinating interrelationship between the Holy Spirit and creation, so that "not only does creation respond to the divine; God also responds for Himself and interacts with the orders of creation,"[32] a circumstance that, by itself, corroborates the assertion of its intrinsic value, independent of human beings.

This does not mean, of course, that this protection, in recognition of the intrinsic value of nature, is not also capable of yielding enormous benefits to humans and society itself. Francis Schaeffer makes a precise statement here, advocating the idea that if we consider nature as having no intrinsic value, our own value is diminished. The depth of this author's insights calls for a transcription:

---

32. Yong, Amos, *O Espírito Derramado sobre a Carne: Pentecostalismo e a Possibilidade de uma Teologia Global* (Campinas: Aldersgate, 2022), p. 412-414.

There is a parallel between the abuse of man towards nature and the abuse of man towards his fellow man. We can see this in two areas. First, let's consider the sexual relationship. What is the attitude of man towards woman? It is possible, and common in the modern scenario, to have an attitude of a 'playboy', or rather, an attitude of treating the 'partner' as a toy. Here, the woman is much more than a sexual object. We have the right to experience pleasure in a sexual relationship, but we have absolutely no right to exploit a partner as a sexual object. There must be a conscious limitation on our pleasure. We impose a limit — a self-imposed limit - in order to honestly treat the wife as a person. So, although a husband is capable of doing more, he does not do everything he is capable of doing because he must also treat her as a person and not simply as a valueless thing. Humanity is lost when he treats the woman as inferior to a human being. Not only her humanity is diminished, but his as well. In contrast, if he does less than what he is capable of doing, in the end, he has more because he has a human relationship: he has love and not just a physical act. *And this is exactly what happens with nature. If we treat nature as hav-*

ing no intrinsic value, our own value is diminished.
A second parallel can be found in a businessman.
I should treat the person I do business with as myself. It is perfectly correct for me to make a profit,
but I should not acquire this profit by treating
him (or exploiting him) as a consumer object. If I
do this, in the end, I will not only destroy him but
myself as well because I will have diminished my
own legitimate value. In the realm of sex and in
the realm of business, treating people as they
should be treated, based on God's creation, is not
only right in itself but produces good results because our own humanity begins to flourish. Now,
both the thing he made and I, who was also made
by him, have wonder, reverence, and real value.
*But we must remember that the value I consciously
place in something will ultimately be my own value
because I too am finite. If I let the wonder escape from
the thing, then the wonder will also escape from the
human race and from myself. And this is where people
live today. All wonder is gone.* Truly, in an arrogant
and selfish way, nature has been reduced to a 'thing'
for man to use and exploit. And if modern man
speaks of protecting the ecological balance of nature, it is only at a pragmatic level for man, without

a basis for nature to have true value in itself. And in this way, man is also reduced in another point of his value, and dehumanized technology takes another turn. We must not allow ourselves individually, nor our technology, to do everything that we or it could be capable of doing. Animals cannot make any conscious limitation. I, who am made in the image of God, can make a choice. As a result, there is beauty instead of a desert. The aesthetic question is also present. Nature surely is something that has importance in itself and should not be underestimated. Beauty does not need pragmatic reasons to have value.[33]

Therefore, contrary to what is commonly propagated, Christianity does not endorse any abuse or disrespect towards nature, viewing it as a mere resource to satisfy the unchecked desires of human beings. Instead, it provides a powerful ethical foundation for the ongoing restraint of human power, legitimizing what is now regarded as sustainable action in the wake of a compassionate anthropocentrism. The exercise of such a perspective, within a deeply interconnected environment, generates benefits not only for nature but also for present and future human beings.

---

33. Schaeffer, Francis, *Poluição e a morte do homem* p. 59-64.

Moderate Use, Earth, and God

It is already evident that in terms of preservation, the sustainability of a system moves in the opposite direction of its ontological reduction. Calvin expresses this perspective when reflecting on the moderate use of the goods found in creation.[34] According to the Geneva reformer, it is necessary to adopt a measure so that we may conscientiously use God's gifts both for delight and necessity. After all, God creates not only for provision but also for rejoicing. In this sense, if we are pilgrims in this world, we should rejoice in the good things that exist as we employ them according to the purpose for which the Author Himself created and intended them.

Jesus Himself bears witness to this perspective. For example, when Jesus performs the miracle of feeding five thousand people with only five barley loaves and two fish, He instructs His disciples to gather the leftover pieces so that nothing is wasted (John 6:12). Even in a context of seemingly unlimited abundance, the gifts of God's creation should not be squandered. We are challenged here to realize that even if we do not experience any crisis related to the use and distribution of resources from our ecosystem, we would

---

34. Calvin, João, *As Institutas* (São Paulo: Editora Cultura Cristã, 2022), p. 78.

still be called to care that reflects our appreciation for the gifts that God bestows.[35]

It is evident that the exercise of dominion is intrinsically linked to service to God; by losing one, humanity inevitably loses the other. Without God, human beings lose their connection with the Earth. Those who have already lost their bond with the Earth have no other way to return to it except through God. From the beginning, humanity's journey toward the Earth has only been possible through God's journey toward humanity. Only when God draws near can we find our way back to the Earth.[36]

In this sense, the notion of God as Lord of Nature provides a harmonious intertwining between the care for creation, represented by human dominion, and the cultural mandate, represented by the development of the potentialities found in creation. Such a symmetrical association is only possible thanks to the fact that the labor over creation will not be exercised in a tyrannical manner but will cherish creational sustainability.

---

35. Moo, Douglas J., Moo, *Jonathan A., Creation Care: A Biblical Theology of the Natural World*, p. 123.

36. Dietrich Bonhoeffer, *Creation and Fall: A Theological Interpretation of Genesis 1-3*, p. 123.

Responsibility and Care

What is intended with this perspective, essentially, as highlighted by Maranhão, is to establish an understanding that allows humans to act with sobriety in the face of the delicate environmental issues that have long demanded critical reflection from us.[37] A vision that, despite recognizing the special human condition compared to other living beings on the planet, as a result, attributes to it not necessarily rights, but rather severe duties conducive to maximum protection and respect not only towards others (including future generations) but also towards everything else that complexly involves and conditions it.

In this way, the valuable freedom of human beings is preserved to pursue their own projects and ideals, while acknowledging their undeniable responsibility to act as wise managers of that which ultimately they know does not belong to them. Based on this perspective, the relationship between humans and nature, as well as the handling of the delicate ecological issue, are therefore seen in the context of an intrinsic ethical demand for responsible management. After all, every allocation of power implies the attraction of responsibilities. In other words, those who have the power to lead have the duty to care. Therefore, in this context, hu-

---

37. Maranhão, Ney, *Poluição Labor-Ambiental*, p. 85.

mans govern the world as a microcosm of God Himself,[38] hence a careful administration of creation emerges as an essential characteristic of biblical *dominium terrae.*[39]

This would be the essence of the redeemed Christian perspective regarding the environmental issue: the relative centrality of humans as the only beings endowed with moral consciousness and capable of choosing not to succumb to any instinctual or impulsive inclination. This centrality involves a two-way street, with some rights granted, but primarily with strict assignment of duties, all permeated by an inherent sense of responsible and sustainable stewardship.

Nevertheless, as John Goldingay emphasizes, from the perspective of authentic Christianity, "being human is a matter of vocation and responsibility towards God and the world, not a matter of rights."[40] Therefore, it is necessary to recognize that only the Christian worldview properly balances these two truths: the radical destruction caused by sin and the hope of complete restoration of the original goodness.[41]

---

38. Naugle, David K., *Filosofia: Um Guia para Estudantes*, p. 61.

39. Volf, Miroslav, *Work in the Spirit: Toward a Theology of Work* (Eugene: Wipf and Stock Publishers, 1991).

40. Goldingay, John, *Teologia Bíblica: O Deus das Escrituras Cristãs* (Rio de Janeiro: Thomas Nelson Brasil, 2020), p.188.

41. Pearcey, Nancy, *Thaxton, Charles, A alma da ciência: fé cristã e filosofia natural*, p. 241.

Thus, adopting the Christian view does not necessarily mean endorsing any abuse or disrespect towards nature or viewing it as a mere source of resources available for the unbridled desires of human beings. Instead, with this perspective expressed here, a powerful ethical foundation is provided for the continuous restraint of human power, legitimizing what is now regarded as sustainable action in the wake of a biblical perspective. Its exercise, which occurs in a deeply interconnected environment, generates benefits not only for nature but also for present and future human beings, expressing a truly conscious and awakened worldview.[42]

It is certain that any discourse on sustainability is essentially an ethical discourse.[43] Therefore, here we are working on establishing ethical and scientific foundations that enable a proper understanding of the environment, life, and the role of humans in the world in which they are placed, considering the fateful "crisis of perception" that overwhelms us at this point in history.[44] Despite scientific

---

42. Maranhão, Ney, *Poluição Labor-Ambiental*, p. 87.

43. Bosselmann, Klaus, *O Princípio da Sustentabilidade: Transformando Direito e Governança* (São Paulo: Editora Revista dos Tribunais, 2015), p. 25

44. Capra, Fritjof, *A Teia da Vida: Uma Nova Compreensão Científica dos Sistemas Vivos* (São Paulo: Editora Cultrix, 2006), p. 23.

naturalism promoting a clash between religion and science, the human need for a unified worldview is surpassing these artificial boundaries.[45]

Thus, in the specific context of the environmental agenda, the redeemed Christian alternative presents itself as an appropriate path to restore the relationship between human beings and nature based on a solid and coherent foundation of meaning. It aligns fully with the international legal framework for environmental protection, given its historical emphasis on the role of humans not only as holders of the right to an ecologically balanced environment but also as directly responsible for the duty to protect and preserve the environment for present and future generations.[46] It should be noted once again that Christianity, despite the ferocity of its critics and their claims of its falsehood, can never be dismissed as intellectually irrelevant.[47]

---

45. Pearcey, Nancy, Thaxton, Charles, *A alma da ciência: fé cristã e filosofia natural*, p. 505.

46. Soares, Vanessa Santos Moreira, "Origens e Perspectivas do Princípio do Desenvolvimento Sustentável" (PhD diss., Programa de Pós-Graduação em Direito Internacional, Faculdade de Direito, Universidade de São Paulo, 2023), p. 163.

47. Pearcey, Nancy, *A Busca da Verdade* (São Paulo: Cultura Cristã, 2018),p. 185.

Universal Calling

Finally, in this regard, let us remember the first promise of redemption in the Bible, that Satan's head would be crushed by the seed of the woman (Gen. 3:15). Undoubtedly, this promise points to our Lord and Savior Jesus Christ, who on the cross gave His life "as a ransom for many" (Mark 10:45), conquering death (1 Cor. 15:55-57) and publicly triumphing over all powers of evil (Col. 2:14-15). In this regard, it is important to add to the reflection what the Holy Spirit revealed to the Apostle Paul in his letter to the Romans, "The God of peace will soon crush Satan under your feet" (Rom. 16:20).

Now, in this occasion, through the text and context, the Spirit clearly stated that Satan would be subdued under the feet of the Church, which, as we know, constitutes the body of Christ (Rom. 12:4-5; 1 Cor. 12:27). Therefore, Calvin correctly interprets the biblical exegesis when he says that in Genesis 3:15, it is not only Christ individually but also the "offspring of the woman in general," so that "the power to crush Satan is communicated to the faithful."[48]

Therefore, caring for creation reveals the importance of every redeemed Christian cultivating and guarding the earth as an inevitable part of what God created us to be. We be-

48. Calvino, *João, Gênesis*, vol. 1 (Recife: Editora CLIRE, 2018), p. 144-145

come powerful instruments in dispelling the evil that dares to embed itself in all of creation due to the Fall. Hence, this theme should not only be a concern for experts.

Indeed, God has called different people to different areas. There are those who have been called to dedicate themselves exclusively to what we can call "creation care," just as there are those who are full-time missionaries, teachers, doctors, or business people. However, caring for creation is fundamentally about becoming who we were created to be, as bearers of the divine image exercising dominion in the created world.

John Stott, in his final book reflecting on the marks that characterize a radical disciple, rightly lists caring for creation as one of the distinctive characteristics of every believer. According to Stott, our work with creation represents a genuine expression of worship and praise since caring for the natural world reflects our love for the Creator.[49] Thus, as the biblical perspective is holistic, meaning for the whole person, we must live in a manner worthy of God's calling in all our attitudes, including our relationship with nature.[50]

---

49. Stott, John, *O Discípulo Radical* (Viçosa: Ultimato, 2021), p. 47.

50. Moo, Douglas J., Moo, *Jonathan A., Creation Care: A Biblical Theology of the Natural World*, p. 86.

4

The Scriptures
and Nature

"But ask now the beasts, and they shall teach thee; And the fowls of the air, and they shall tell thee: Or speak to the earth, and it shall teach thee: And the fishes of the sea shall declare unto thee. Who knoweth not in all these That the hand of the LORD hath wrought this? In whose hand *is* the soul of every living thing, And the breath of all mankind" (Job 12.7-10).

SEVERAL BIBLICAL TEXTS, BOTH from the Old and New Testaments, written in multiple styles and varied contexts, reflect God's care for creation. In addition to the verses already mentioned, this final section intentionally examines other passages with the purpose of deepening, in the light of Scripture, the real foundation of human care and responsibility regarding nature, that is, its importance to the Creator.

Jesus, Sparrows, and Lilies

Jesus demonstrates a deep connection and special attention to the natural world around Him. His teachings in the rural settings of first-century Galilee often use imagery related to agriculture, such as farms, farmers, vineyards, seeds, fishing, trees, flowers, and birds. His teachings are delivered mainly outdoors, by the seashore, in boats, on mountains, and in green fields. Following Jesus' example reminds us of the beauty and richness present in the world created by God and reconnects us with our true identity as created beings, part of a marvelous creation under God's sovereign rule in Christ. After all, we are all part of creation and intimately connected, receiving our life from God's creative act, whether we acknowledge it or not.[1]

In the Gospels, we glimpse the value that Jesus places on the natural world and the appreciation of its beauty. Against the concerns of this life, for example, Jesus uses God's care for sparrows to reassure His disciples about the Father's care for them, "Are not two sparrows sold for a penny? Yet not one of them will fall to the ground outside your Father's

---

1. Moo, Douglas J., Moo, Jonathan A., *Creation Care: A Biblical Theology of the Natural*, p. 121.

care. And even the very hairs of your head are all numbered. So don't be afraid; you are worth more than many sparrows!" (Matthew 10:29-31).

If God has intimate knowledge and care for sparrows, then the care He has for us is even greater. As J. C. Ryle mentions, if the Creator of all things provides food to satisfy the needs of the birds in the sky, so that they have a daily provision of food, surely we should not fear.[2] Thus, Jesus reaffirms that "you are worth more than many sparrows" (Luke 12:24), providing us with a solid foundation to recognize the unique value of human life. However, the foundation of Jesus' message depends on the fact that sparrows also have value and importance before God, and all are worthy of His care.

Jesus also uses the beauty and abundance of nature to show His disciples that God will provide for them. "Consider how the wild flowers grow. They do not labor or spin. Yet I tell you, not even Solomon in all his splendor was dressed like one of these" (Luke 12:27). Jesus instructs His followers to contemplate the natural world, appreciate its beauty, and draw lessons from it—about the nature of the Creator God and the response we should have.[3]

---

2. Ryle, J. C., *Meditações no Evangelho de Lucas* (São José dos Campos: Editora Fiel, 2013), p. 218.

3. Moo, Douglas J., Moo, Jonathan A., *Creation Care: A Biblical Theology of the Natural*, p. 121.

Indeed, worry prevents us from seeing the world around us and how God cares for His creation. God has given beauty to the lilies and food to the birds, which cannot sow or reap. Therefore, He will provide for His children all things. In this case, the appropriate response is to abandon anxiety about our personal needs and not to worry excessively: "If God clothes the grass of the field, which today exists and tomorrow is thrown into the fire, how much more will he clothe you, men of little faith!" (Luke 12:28).[4]

The example of Jesus with the lilies and the ravens, mentioned earlier, is intended to dispel the fear and anxiety that often lead to selfish concerns, greed, and reluctance to be generous. In contrast, Jesus reminds His disciples that the heavenly Father knows all their needs and is capable of providing abundantly: "But seek first His kingdom and His righteousness, and all these things will be given to you as well. Therefore, do not worry about tomorrow, for tomorrow will worry about itself. Each day has enough trouble of its own" (Matthew 6:33-34).[5]

---

4. Wiersbe, Warren, *Comentário Bíblico Expositivo: Novo Testamento I* (Santo André: Geográfica, 2014), p. 288.

5. Moo, Douglas J., Moo, Jonathan A., *Creation Care: A Biblical Theology of the Natural*, p. 122.

Greed, Passivity, and Reproof

In addition to advising His disciples on the daily goodness and sovereignty of God, Jesus also took time to warn them about the dangers of pride and fear, using pastoral context figures.

The greedy spirit of the human heart is vividly revealed in Jesus' parable about the rich fool (Luke 12:13-21). Having received the divine gift of a great harvest, the man had no more room to store his crops. Reasoning with himself, he decides, "I will tear down my barns and build bigger ones, and there I will store my surplus grain. And I will say to myself, 'You have plenty of grain laid up for many years. Take life easy; eat, drink and be merry'" (Luke 12:18-19).

However, his monologue is suddenly interrupted by the voice of the Lord, which resonates like a terrible thunderclap, saying, "You fool! This very night your life will be demanded from you. Then who will get what you have prepared for yourself?" (Luke 12:20). The man's life plan was revealed as foolish: more money; more goods; and more joy. Thus, as his harvest and goods had been given by the Lord, now his soul is also required, for his life does not belong to him.

The central point of this parable is not the discovery of death—everyone knows they will die someday—but the reality that:

i. everything that exists belongs to the Lord;

ii. we are only stewards of divine gifts;

iii. the pride that generates the greedy impulse of the human heart is insatiable; and

iv. everyone will have to give an account of how they manage what was granted by God Himself.[6] Thus, there is no reason to think that caring for creation is not included in the list of human responsibilities that will one day be required of the servants by the Lord.

Just as in the parable of the rich fool, the parable of the talents (Luke 19:11-27) also reveals to the church the need to prudently manage the goods granted by God. Having gone to a distant country to be made king, the nobleman gave his servants sums of money to trade while he was away. However, the community where the servants were located was rebellious and did not want the nobleman to reign over them.

In this hostile environment, faithfulness was required of the servants to invest and develop publicly the assets entrusted to them by the Lord. As the parable continues, one of the three servants simply kept what was given to him inoperative, and he

---

6.   Bailey, Kenneth, *Jesus pela Ótica do Oriente Médio: Estudos Culturais sobre os Evangelhos* (São Paulo: Vida Nova, 2016), p. 300.

was reprimanded when his master returned, who also took away from the servant everything that had been assigned to him.

We can see that the parable is not about successful investments. On the contrary, the teaching that Jesus aims to convey through the story revolves around the understanding that: i) the Lord's main expectation of His servants is public and courageous faithfulness to an invisible Lord at the present moment, even amidst persecution and hostility.[7] Thus, the inactive conservation of God's gifts is treason against the One who grants them.

Just as seen in the other parable, a faithful steward is required not only to refrain from greed or passivity regarding goods but also to take careful care and cultivate what has been entrusted to him by his Lord (Genesis 2:15).

Sabbath Rest and Jubilee Year

The law given by God specifically to the people of Israel contains relevant principles for all people throughout all times. For example, in opposition to the greedy impulses of the human heart and in pursuit of rest in the presence of the Lord, the Sabbath prescription is established early in the history of the Exodus. The fourth commandment states: "But the seventh day is the Sabbath of the Lord your God; in it

---

7.   Bailey, Kenneth, *Jesus pela Ótica do Oriente Médio: Estudos Culturais sobre os Evangelhos*, 408.

you shall not do any work: you, nor your son, nor your daughter, nor your male servant, nor your female servant, nor your cattle, nor your stranger who is within your gates" (Exodus 20:10).

The biblical text emphasizes that not only the Israelites or foreigners should observe the seventh day, but also their animals: "Six days you shall do your work, and on the seventh day you shall rest, that your ox and your donkey may rest…" (Exodus 23:12). Regarding the care of the land, God also commands the nation of Israel to observe the seventh year: "Six years you shall sow your field, and six years you shall prune your vineyard, and gather its fruit; but in the seventh year there shall be a Sabbath of solemn rest for the land, a Sabbath to the Lord…" (Leviticus 25:3-4).[8]

Furthermore, the institution of the Jubilee year also had similar purposes. The divine command emphasized that every fiftieth year should be a period of liberation and restoration. In the Jubilee year, the land would not be cultivated, and the debts of the poor would be canceled. The land itself was to be redistributed so that no one would amass excessive wealth at the expense of their brothers. God emphasizes, "The land shall not be sold

8. Chester, *Tim, Êxodo para Você* (São Paulo: Vida Nova, 2019), 190.

permanently, for the land is Mine; for you are strangers and sojourners with Me" (Leviticus 25:23).

In this way, we can perceive that even though the Lord had granted the land to Israel as a grace to be enjoyed, it still belonged to the Lord, and the people were only like tenants whose lives and work should serve God Himself. The principles found in the ancient commandments given to the people of Israel prescribe the need to rest in divine sovereignty, reject the unrestrained desire for more material possessions, and respect, as faithful stewards, the animals and the land, which belong to God.

Jonah's Rebellion and God's Mercy

The book of Jonah uniquely intertwines God's sovereignty and love, presenting God both as the Creator of all things—"the God of heaven, who made the sea and the dry land" (Jonah 1:9)—and as the One who reigns in power when obeyed by all of the natural world (Jonah 1:4, 1:15, 1:17; 2:10). Despite the prophet's disobedience in not preaching, as ordered by the Lord (Jonah 1:2), repentance by the people of the city of Nineveh led God to have mercy on Jonah and to send the great fish (Jonah 1:17). Repentant, the prophet preaches, and the city turns to God in sackcloth and ashes (Jonah 3:6). In grace, God forgives the Ninevites. Dissatisfied, Jonah leaves the city to see what would actually happen (Jonah 4:5), namely, whether the city would face divine judgment.

Continuing the biblical narrative, we see that, expecting the city's destruction in the heat, God causes a plant to grow to provide shade for Jonah, who greatly rejoices in the relief (Jonah 4:6). However, God sends a worm to eat the plant, causing it to wither and bringing back intense heat to the prophet, who murmurs (Jonah 4:7-9).

God then says, "You have had pity on the plant for which you have not labored, nor made it grow, which came up in a night and perished in a night. And should I not pity Nineveh, that great city, in which are more than one hundred and twenty thousand persons who cannot discern between their right hand and their left—and much livestock?" (Jonah 4:10-11).

It wasn't the greatness or fame of Nineveh that moved His compassion. God provides two reasons in this rhetorical question to spare the city. First, there were more than one hundred and twenty thousand people who lacked discernment, meaning the Lord does not delight in the death of the sinner (Ezekiel 18:21-23). Second, there were also many animals. It's interesting that the text mentions animal life as one of the reasons for preserving the city, revealing what we have been analyzing throughout this study: God cares about His creation.

"Where Were You, Job?"

The final chapters of the book of Job express the grandeur of God's wisdom and power through the beauties and depths involved in creation. Up to this point, despite all of Job's suffering, anguish, fear, and questioning, God remained silent. While readers of this biblical book possess discernment about the higher purposes of God to be achieved through what Job had experienced, Job had no awareness of this reality.

It's interesting to note that the Lord doesn't mention anything about the reason for Job's suffering, redirecting all attention to His dominion and authority manifested in the creation and sustenance of nature. Through the description of the natural world, God shows Job that His plans are beyond human comprehension and that His actions are far beyond any human's capacity to fully understand. Nature is a tangible expression of God's creative power, and His control over it demonstrates His authority over everything that exists.

For example, in the midst of the storm, the Lord questions Job with a series of rhetorical questions: "Where were you when I laid the foundations of the earth? Tell Me, if you have understanding" (Job 38:4); "Upon what were its foundations fastened, or who laid its cornerstone, when the morning stars sang together, and all the sons of God shouted for joy?" (Job 38:6-7); "Have you commanded the morning since your days began, and caused the dawn to know its place, that it might take hold of the ends of the earth, and the wicked be shaken out of it?" (Job 38:12-13); and "Shall you hunt the prey for the lion, or satisfy the appetite of the young lions, when they crouch in their dens, or lurk in their lairs to lie in wait?" (Job 38:39-40).

Through these questions, God describes the magnificence and complexity of the natural world, mentioning the mysteries of the stars, the origin of thunder, the birth and instincts of animals. By doing so, God reveals His authority as the Creator, who designed and rules over all aspects of the natural world. By revealing the grandeur of creation, God also invites Job to recognize his own limitations and dependence on God.[9]

This realization leads Job to repent and submit to God's will, understanding that even amidst suffering and apparent injustice, God is sovereign and wise in His purposes. Job, as an example to all of us, humbles himself by saying, "I am

---

9.   Moo, Douglas J., Moo, Jonathan A., *Creation Care: A Biblical Theology of the Natural*, p. 62.

vile; what shall I answer You? I lay my hand over my mouth" (Job 40:4).

Thus, the narrative concludes with Job experiencing restoration and blessing from God, showing that those who humble themselves before divine power are sustained by His grace and mercy. After all, following the same conclusion directed by Jesus (Matthew 10:29-31), if God cares for His vast creation in the described manner, would He not also care for Job's suffering?

Divine Providence to All Creatures

Psalm 104 is perhaps the most beautiful manifestation of praise to the Creator God found in the pages of the Scriptures. The Psalm begins and ends with expressions of exaltation to God for His glory and majesty, permeated with extravagant details of the richness of the natural world. Its author "turns the truth of creation into a song and environmental theory into wonder and praise."[10] As emphasized earlier, the God presented in the Bible is not the god of deists, who believe that the world was divinely created but left on its own thereafter. On the contrary, the Lord creates and sustains all of His creation.

---

10. Carson, D. A., et al., *Comentário Bíblico Vida Nova* (São Paulo: Vida Nova, 2009), p. 836.

God provides water to the animals and the earth, causing food to grow:

"You make springs gush forth in the valleys;
they flow between the hills; they give drink to every beast
    of the field;
the wild donkeys quench their thirst.
Beside them the birds of the heavens dwell;
    they sing among the branches.
From Your lofty abode, You water the mountains; the earth
    is satisfied with the fruit of Your work"
    (Psalm 104:10-13).

In truth, the very existence of life depends entirely on His presence:

"When You hide Your face, they are dismayed;
when You take away their breath, they die and return to
    their dust.
When You send forth Your Spirit, they are created, and You
    renew the face of the ground" (Psalm 104:29-30).

This Psalm is interesting because it explicitly conveys the fact that God cares not only about human civilization but also takes interest and delight in all of creation. Indeed, God provides for humanity:

"You cause the grass to grow for the livestock and plants
    for man to cultivate,

that he may bring forth food from the earth,
and wine to gladden the heart of man,
oil to make his face shine and bread to strengthen
man's heart" (Psalm 104:14-15).

However, in the same way, He provides even for the wildest corners of creation, such as the animals that roam the wilderness (Psalm 104:20). Verse 24 of the Psalm concludes as an appropriate interpretative key, encouraging us to celebrate the magnificent creation made by God:

"O Lord, how manifold are Your works!
In wisdom have You made them all;
the earth is full of Your creatures" (Psalm 104:24).[11]

---

11. Moo, Douglas J., Moo, Jonathan A., *Creation Care: A Biblical Theology of the Natural*, p. 59.

Conclusion

"O LORD, how manifold are thy works!
In wisdom hast thou made them all:
The earth is full of thy riches" (Ps 104.24).

FROM A MULTIDISCIPLINARY APPROACH, intertwining Philosophy and Theology, we seek in this essay, without any pretense of exhausting the topic, to expose the biblical perspective on the relationship that should exist between humanity and nature. Through cultural analysis, we observe that many Christians ignore the need to care for creation, considering it inferior, as a domain exclusively reserved for movements antagonistic to scriptural principles, or as a secondary concern compared to debates about how God created the universe. However, as we emphasize, inactivity is not a valid option as it leads to secularization and dishonors the divine commandment of stewardship. Likewise, we should not deify nature.

Next, we deem unfounded the scientific criticism that Christianity is the source of the existing ecological crisis in the world. Any perspective rooted in this premise results from a misconstrued understanding of Christian precepts and commandments. As we have seen, the terms "subject," "dominate," "cultivate," and "guard" do not imply destructive mandates; rather, they reflect the need for humanity to exercise stewardship and balance toward creation. As analyzed, creaturely dominion does not imply sovereignty but rather emphasizes the need for responsible and sustainable use of earthly resources.

In reality, we emphasize that the true origin of the environmental crisis stems from human original rebellion, which distorts the understanding of caring for nature. Divine ordinances are distorted, and humanity contemplates the God/Nature relationship in various misguided ways, which can be summarized as follows: God identified with nature, God above nature, and God separated from nature. All of these perspectives are problematic as they fail to offer plausible moral justifications for their positions and, consequently, fail to preserve creation adequately and effectively.

Therefore, in order to propose a solution to the environmental problem, we seek to interpret human interaction with the environment through the redemptive lens proposed by Scripture. In His sovereign and majestic way, God creates all things out of nothing for the praise of His glory, granting humanity the creative dominion and cultural mandate. However, what does biblical restoration applied to creation mean after the Fall and the existence of sin?

If Christ is the Lord of all human existence, we assert that His redemption should promote restoration in all areas of life, including human beings' relationship with the created world. We present the view of God as the Lord of nature, which aims to represent a redeemed alternative to the human-nature relationship. This understanding, rooted in the biblical concept of dominion that humans should exercise over creation (Genesis 1:26-28 and 2:15; Psalm 8:5-6), not only brings forth various positive aspects but also establishes the foundation for caring for creation. It stems from the fact that God, out of love, created all things and cares for them, demanding that human beings faithfully act as His vice-regents on Earth.

We emphasize, therefore, that biblically, man has dominion but not sovereignty. His dominion is functionalized for purposes higher than himself, not allowing any degree or measure of degradation, undue exploitation, or abuse, as man's dominion will only be legitimate if and when practiced in fidelity to God's dominion. Thus, we do not embrace a view marked by the inviolability of nature. On the contrary, we advocate for a necessary and beneficial synergy between human beings and the environment, activating mutual potentialities and generating reciprocal benefits, to the extent that it also enables man, as an astute representative of the Creator of the Universe, to engage with the richness of the natural world for his own benefit (nutritionally, residentially, technologically, aesthetically, poetically, etc.), without inherently committing sin in doing so.

However, from this perspective, the relationship between man and nature and the approach to the delicate environmental issue must always be viewed within a context of an intrinsic ethical requirement for responsible management. Here, the centrality of the human role is not exclusively about the entitlement to rights, but primarily about the strict assignment of duties, demanding a loving and responsible approach in his dealings with creation.

Under this hopeful Christian perspective, nature is respected because it possesses intrinsic value given by God Himself. At the same time, it is not experienced through an exploitative, intangible, or even sacred relationship, as is customary in apostate worldviews. Finally, we affirm that the Christian perspective stands as the only one that allows human beings, through responsible stewardship, to seek to restore harmony between the creational orders of dominion and cultural mandate in society. This provides solid and appropriate ethical and scientific foundations for the realization of sustainable development of creation.

Bibliography

Allison, Gregg R. 2017. *Teologia histórica: Uma introdução ao desenvolvimento da doutrina cristã*. São Paulo: Vida Nova.

Augustine, Saint. 2018. *On Faith, Hope, and Love (The Enchiridion): The Early Church Father's Christian Teachings on Prayer and Piety*. [S.l.]: Adansonia Publishing.

Barth, Karl. 1969. *Church Dogmatics*. Vol. 3. Edinburgh: T&T Clark.

Bavinck, Herman. 2021. *As maravilhas de Deus*. Rio de Janeiro: Thomas Nelson Brasil.

Beltrão, Antônio Figueiredo Guerra. 2014. *Curso de direito ambiental*. 2nd ed. São Paulo: Método.

Bonhoeffer, Dietrich. 1959. *Creation and Fall: A Theological Interpretation of Genesis 1–3*. London: SCM.

Bosselmann, Klaus. 2015. *O princípio da sustentabilidade: Transformando direito e governança*. São Paulo: Editora Revista dos Tribunais.

Bratt, James D. 1988. *Sphere Sovereignty*. Grand Rapids, MI: Eerdmans.

Calvino, João. 2015. *Epístolas Gerais*. São José dos Campos: Fiel.

Calvino, João. 2018. *Gênesis*. Vol. 1. Recife: Editora CLIRE.

Calvino, João. 2022. *As Institutas*. São Paulo: Editora Cultura Cristã.

Camus, Albert. 1945. *Le mythe de Sisyphe*. Paris: Gallimard.

Campos, Heber Carlos de. 2011. *O habitat humano: O paraíso criado*. São Paulo: Hagnos.

Campos Jr., Heber. 2019. *Amando a Deus no mundo: Por uma cosmovisão reformada*. São José dos Campos, SP: Fiel.

Capra, Fritjof. 2006. *A teia da vida: Uma nova compreensão científica dos sistemas vivos*. São Paulo: Editora Cultrix.

Carson, D. A., et al. 2009. *Comentário Bíblico Vida Nova*. São Paulo: Vida Nova.

Chester, Tim. 2019. *Êxodo para você*. São Paulo: Vida Nova.

Colson, Charles, and Nancy Pearcey. 2005. *E agora, como viveremos?* 3rd ed. Rio de Janeiro: CPAD.

Descartes, René. 1983. *Discurso do método*. 3rd ed. São Paulo: Abril Cultural.

Dooyeweerd, Herman. 1969. *A New Critique of Theoretical Thought: The Necessary Presuppositions of Philosophy*. Vol. 1. Philadelphia: Presbyterian and Reformed Publishing Co.

Dooyeweerd, Herman. 2010. *No crepúsculo do pensamento ocidental*. São Paulo: Hagnos.

Dooyeweerd, Herman. 2015. *Raízes da cultura ocidental*. São Paulo: Cultura Cristã.

Frame, John. 2013. *A doutrina da vida cristã*. São Paulo: Cultura Cristã.

Goldingay, John. 2020. *Teologia bíblica: O Deus das escrituras cristãs*. Rio de Janeiro: Thomas Nelson Brasil.

Gomes, Carla Amado. 2010. *Direito ambiental: O ambiente como objeto e os objetos do direito do ambiente*. Curitiba: Juruá.

Grudem, Wayne. 1999. *Teologia sistemática*. São Paulo: Vida Nova.

Horton, Michael. 2016. *Doutrinas da fé cristã: Uma teologia sistemática para os peregrinos no caminho*. São Paulo: Cultura Cristã.

Kenneth, Bailey. 2016. *Jesus pela ótica do Oriente Médio: Estudos culturais sobre os Evangelhos*. São Paulo: Vida Nova.

Kidner, Derek. 1979. *Gênesis: Introdução e comentário*. São Paulo: Vida Nova.

Lewis, C. S. 2005. *A abolição do homem*. São Paulo: Martins Fontes.

Lewis, C. S. 2009. *Cristianismo puro e simples*. 3rd ed. São Paulo: Editora WMF Martins Fontes.

Maranhão, Ney. 2017. *Poluição labor-ambiental*. Rio de Janeiro: Lumen Juris.

Milaré, Édis. 2014. *Direito do ambiente*. 9th ed. São Paulo: Editora Revista dos Tribunais.

Moo, Douglas J. 2006. "Nature in the New Creation: New Testament Eschatology and the Environment." *Journal of the Evangelical Theological Society* 49 (3): 449.

Moo, Douglas J., and Jonathan A. Moo. 2018. *Creation Care: A Biblical Theology of the Natural World*. Grand Rapids, MI: Zondervan Academic.

Naugle, David K. 2018. *Filosofia: Um guia para estudantes*. Brasília: Editora Monergismo.

Ost, François. 1995. *A natureza à margem da lei: A ecologia à prova do direito*. Lisboa: Instituto Piaget.

Pearcey, Nancy. 2018. *A busca da verdade*. São Paulo: Cultura Cristã.

Pearcey, Nancy, and Charles Thaxton. 2005. *A alma da ciência: Fé cristã e filosofia natural*. São Paulo: Cultura Cristã.

Piper, John. 2022. *Providência*. São José dos Campos: Fiel.

Plantinga Jr., Cornelius. 2007. *O crente no mundo de Deus*. São Paulo: Cultura Cristã.

Queiroz, Leonardo Balena, and Ney Maranhão. 2023. *Faith and Sustainability: A Christian Contribution to the Issue of Environmental Preservation*. Findings, Issue 5, June. Dunedin, New Zealand: Thumbwidth Press.

Queiroz, Sérgio Augusto de. 2016. "O direito ambiental e a cosmovisão judaico-cristã." In *Direito e cristianismo: Temas atuais e polêmicos*, edited by Abner de Cássio Ferreira, Antonio Carlos da Rosa Silva Júnior, Glauco Barreira Magalhães Filho, Ney Maranhão, and Rodolfo Pamplona Filho, vol. 2. Rio de Janeiro: Editora Betel.

Rookmaaker, H. R. 2010. *A arte não precisa de justificativa*. Viçosa: Ultimato.

Rookmaaker, H. R. 2018. *O dom criativo*. Brasília: Monergismo.

Rubio, A. García. 1992. "Crise ambiental e projeto bíblico de humanização integral." In *Reflexão cristã sobre o meio ambiente*, edited by A. García Rubio et al. São Paulo: Edições Loyola.

Ryle, J. C. 2013. *Meditações no Evangelho de Lucas*. São José dos Campos: Editora Fiel.

Schaeffer, Francis. 2003. *Poluição e a morte do homem*. São Paulo: Cultura Cristã.

Schaeffer, Francis. 2016. *O Deus que intervém*. São Paulo: Cultura Cristã.

Schaeffer, Francis. 2017. *O Deus que se revela*. São Paulo: Cultura Cristã.

Scruton, Roger. 2016. *Filosofia Verde: Como pensar seriamente o planeta*. São Paulo: É Realizações.

Singer, Peter. 2002. *Vida ética*. Rio de Janeiro: Ediouro.

Soares, Vanessa Santos Moreira. 2023. "Origens e perspectivas do princípio do desenvolvimento sustentável." PhD diss., Faculdade de Direito, Universidade de São Paulo.

Stoll, Mark R. 2015. *Inherit the Holy Mountain: Religion and the Rise of American Environmentalism*. New York: Oxford University Press.

Stott, John. 2021. *O discípulo radical*. Viçosa: Ultimato.

Volf, Miroslav. 1991. *Work in the Spirit: Toward a Theology of Work*. Eugene, OR: Wipf and Stock Publishers.

Walton, John H. 2016. *O mundo perdido de Adão e Eva: O debate sobre a origem da humanidade e a leitura de Gênesis*. Viçosa: Ultimato.

White Jr., Lynn. 1967. "The Historical Roots of Our Ecologic Crisis." *Science* 155 (3767): 1203–1207.

Wiersbe, Warren. 2014. *Comentário Bíblico Expositivo: Novo Testamento I*. Santo André: Geográfica.

Williams, J. Rodman. 2011. *Teologia sistemática: Uma perspectiva pentecostal*. São Paulo: Editora Vida.

Wolters, Albert M. 2019. *A criação restaurada: A base bíblica para uma cosmovisão reformada*. São Paulo: Cultura Cristã.

Wright, N. T. 2009. *Surpreendido pela esperança*. Viçosa: Ultimato.

Yong, Amos. 2022. *O Espírito derramado sobre a carne: Pentecostalismo e a possibilidade de uma teologia global*

ABOUT THE CÁNTARO INSTITUTE
Inheriting, Informing, Inspiring

Cántaro Institute is a reformed evangelical organization committed to advancing the Christian worldview for the reformation and renewal of the church and culture.

We believe that as the Christian church returns to the fount of the Scriptures as its ultimate authority for all knowledge and life, and wisely applies God's truth to every aspect of life, its missiological activity will result not only in the renewal of the human person but also in the reformation of culture—an inevitable outcome when the true scope and nature of the gospel are made known and applied.